ZAMBA.

Painted by F.Simpson.　　　　　　　　　Engraved by E.Finden

AFRICAN NEGRO SLAVE.

LIFE AND ADVENTURES
OF
ZAMBA,

AN AFRICAN NEGRO KING;
AND HIS EXPERIENCE OF
SLAVERY IN SOUTH CAROLINA

WRITTEN BY HIMSELF

Corrected and Arranged By
PETER NEILSON

The Black Heritage Library Collection

 BOOKS FOR LIBRARIES PRESS
FREEPORT, NEW YORK
1970

First Published 1847
Reprinted 1970

Reprinted from a copy in the
Fisk University Library Negro Collection

INTERNATIONAL STANDARD BOOK NUMBER:
0-8369-8717-9

LIBRARY OF CONGRESS CATALOG CARD NUMBER:
70-133162

PRINTED IN THE UNITED STATES OF AMERICA

London:
Printed by STEWART and MURRAY.
Old Bailey.

EDITOR'S PREFACE.

In presenting to the British Public the Autobiography of a Negro Slave, it may be expected of me, as Editor, to state the circumstances under which this narrative came into my hands, and my reasons for believing that it is really what it professes to be, namely, The Life, Adventures, and Experiences of an African Prince, named Zamba, who succeeded his father as the King of a small territory on the banks of the Congo, and who was inveigled by the captain of an American slaver, and sold as a slave at Charleston, in South Carolina.

This I am willing to do for the sake of truth and justice, although, in thus publicly avowing my participation in Zamba's attacks upon slavery and slave-owners, I am quite aware that I shall provoke the displeasure of many individuals now resident in

a

Charleston, whom I regard as my personal friends,
and, no doubt, I shall also incur the odium of all
who are in favour of the continuance of negro slavery.

I could not comply with the request of the Publishers of the work, that I would afford them an
opportunity of communicating directly with Zamba;
for (though it may not be generally known in this
country) a letter addressed to a coloured person in
Charleston by his proper name, would be opened at
the post-office of that city, and in such a case as the
present, Zamba's life would not be worth an hour's
purchase.

I therefore do not hesitate to declare, that I
was personally acquainted with the African negro
named Zamba, whose history is here related; and
that, during a residence of several years in Charleston, I heard from his own lips the leading incidents
of his life. I have therefore no doubt of the truth
of the statements contained in this narrative; indeed, as regards the occurrences in Charleston, some
anecdotes are too well known in that city to be
controverted.

That Zamba received considerable assistance in
writing his autobiography, from both white and
coloured friends, he himself states in his Preface;

and I think it right to avow, that my duties as Editor have not been limited to merely verbal revision. As the friend of Zamba, I felt myself at liberty to aid, in common with his friends in Charleston, in rendering his narrative more full and attractive, by introducing remarks that he had made to me, and giving greater effect to some passages of description. I have also taken upon myself to sanction the omission of certain portions of no particular interest in relation to Zamba and slavery. I should have had some scruples in making any alteration whatever in Zamba's narrative, had it been wholly and solely his own composition, however rude; and I agree with the Publishers in wishing that the statements of this poor African had been written throughout in his own phraseology. This not being the case, however, I can only hope that since I have done nothing but what I had warrant for doing, the truthful character of the narrative has not been lessened by any act of mine, and that the inherent evidences of its authenticity will be recognised and felt by the reader; for I can truly state, that in all essential points this narrative is genuine and authentic.

It may be proper to add, that I shall have no

objection to give, to any sincere and candid inquirer for truth's sake, such further information as may be desired to satisfy any reasonable person of the reality of the hero of this autobiography—short of affording any' clue to the identification of Zamba: for that would expose him to persecution, if not to the deadly vengeance of the slave-holders in the white community amongst which he resides.

PETER NEILSON.

Kirkintilloch, North Britain,
March 1847.

PREFACE BY THE AUTHOR.

It will no doubt be deemed a strange circumstance that an African negro should attempt to write a book, and that he should presume to offer his production to the enlightened people of Great Britain.

When, however, it is understood that, in the country in which he resides—the so-called free States of America—certain laws totally debar him from appearing before the public as an author, he will perhaps be the more readily excused for availing himself of the freedom of the press of England, the only country upon earth where true and genuine liberty has taken up her abode.

It may, perhaps, be a new thing to many persons, even in Britain, to know, that the laws of the state of South Carolina, in which I reside, are such, that the printer who would be rash enough to print, or the bookseller who would be daring enough to offer for sale, the production of a negro, or any work written on behalf of this oppressed race, would not

only draw upon himself the strong hand of the
law, in the shape of a ruinous penalty, but would
be exposed to the fury and summary vengeance of
an insulted republic.   Were a single copy of this
simple production of mine to appear for sale in the
window of any shopkeeper in the city of Charleston,
a short time only would elapse ere the " Sovereign
People" would attack the house and the person of
the unfortunate trader, armed with all the horrors
of " Lynch law,"—a law which now proverbially
reflects so much honour and credit on the mighty
western republic.   Tarring and feathering, and,
finally, hanging from the nearest lamp-post, would
be considered proper treatment for the rash bookseller ; but were it discovered that a wretched negro
was at the bottom of the affair, he would probably
be torn limb from limb, as a warning and example
to his black brethren.

Under these circumstances, it will be said that I
might have brought out my book in some of the
really free states of America—New York, for instance.   I may mention, however, that although
many States in the Union do not actually *hold* slaves
themselves, there yet exists, generally speaking, a
strong and deep-rooted prejudice against the black
race.   And since Providence has put it in my
power, I prefer going at once to the fountain-head
of liberty, and imploring the sympathy and the

succour of that truly great nation, whose common
people, as they may be called, at a mighty sacrifice
of their own interests and those of their posterity, a
few years ago, by one simultaneous and magnani-
mous act, burst the fetters of eight hundred thousand of their fellow-subjects, residing in far distant
parts of the earth. Such a people, understanding
the real condition of nearly three millions of slaves in
the United States, cannot, and I am sure will not,
refuse their sympathy to the cause of the much
wronged Negro.

My great ambition in writing this book is, to add
fuel to the heavenly fire of humane and Christian
feeling which already exists in the hearts of Britain's
free-born sons towards the oppressed slave ; and
should I succeed in creating any additional interest
in behalf of my proscribed race, happy indeed shall
I deem myself. Even the very thought that I have,
in a small degree, made the actual condition of the
poor negro more clear and palpable, will be a great
satisfaction to me.

It will naturally be inquired,—" By what means
have you acquired the requisite education to fit you
for your present attempt ? " Should the courteous
reader indulge me by a perusal of the following
pages, he will be informed on the subject. This
much, however, I may say, that I have had the
advice and the partial assistance, as I have pro-

ceeded with my labours, of two or three coloured
friends — men who have travelled in Europe and
other parts of the world, and who possess talents
and education which might confer honour even
upon a white man. I have also had the advice and
approbation of a white friend or two, who feel an
interest in the cause of humanity, and who do not
consider themselves utterly contaminated by occasional friendly intercourse with a black man.

Although I have had many misgivings in regard
to my present attempt, I yet derive considerable
spirit and encouragement from the idea, that, as
the production of an African negro, it will excite in
Christian England, even a larger share of interest
and sympathy than were it the production of an
educated white man; for negro authors are, no
doubt, scarce in the world: but I am aware that
I must not be too sanguine on this point. It is
my conviction, however, that in this city of Charleston, there are many of my oppressed and vilified
race, who could produce a book, not only equal,
but superior to this; had they only enjoyed the
same opportunities of education and information
as have fallen to my lot.

In the course of these pages, I have introduced
a few topics not immediately connected with negro
slavery. I humbly trust, however, that the indulgent reader will not find such paragraphs

altogether void of interest; on the contrary, I hope
that he may find a few novelties, and become
interested in my narrative.

For very obvious reasons, I have been obliged
to give fictitious names to the persons mentioned
in the several anecdotes related; not wishing un-
necessarily to harass the feelings even of those
who, by their conduct, evince a want of regard
for the dearest and holiest rights of mankind. For
my own safety, also, and that of my friends, I have
been obliged to use great caution, lest any clue
might be taken hold of to trace out and persecute
us, for our presumption in daring to say, or even
to think, that freedom is the natural birthright of
all men everywhere upon the face of the earth.

I have interested *one* white gentleman, especially
in my favour, and to him, I trust, I shall never be
deficient in gratitude. May I venture to hope that
the general cause of liberty may, in a certain degree,
be advanced through his means. It is through him
that these pages are destined to appear in type.
He has undertaken to forward my manuscript to
a friend in Britain, who will take the matter in
hand; and it will, indeed, be a happy day for me
when a copy shall reach my hands. It is not one
copy, no, nor fifty copies, I fondly hope, that will
suffice for Charleston. I even anticipate that some
copies will be sought for by the enemies of liberty.

There is no doubt that some of our high-minded
and domineering planters and slave-dealers will be
curious to see what " the black rascal" has dared to
say of his betters. How they will fume and fret;
ay, and curse and blaspheme! They will offer
rewards of dollars by the hundred, and perhaps by
the thousand, to discover who Zamba is; but I
calculate, as the Yankees express it, that Zamba is
beyond the reach of their malice and fury.

I feel thus far sanguine, because I am convinced
that ere another generation pass away, American
slavery will be on its last legs. And can any
man, white or black, breathe a warmer prayer for
America, than to wish that ere long she may, in
truth and in deed, be as free from the curse and
contamination of slavery, in every shape, as her
high-souled and glorious mother, Britain.

And now, courteous reader, I crave your indul-
gence in perusing the following pages. Consider,
in the first place, the situation and condition of the
author, and make every allowance which your good
nature will suffer you to do, in behalf of his inex-
perience, his limited education, and that natural
incapability of any intellectual effort which has
hitherto (at least by a large proportion of white men)
been supposed inseparable from the African race.
In the next place, consider the cause in which I am
writing; and if a British heart beat within your

bosom, I may rest content, that for the cause of human-kind in general, you will make great allowance for my deficiencies. Lastly, pardon my presumption; consider, that possibly Providence may have singled me out from my brethren, and enabled me thus to embody my thoughts, for the purpose of arousing a flame which, although feeble and glimmering, may yet grow brighter and brighter, until the hearts and consciences of all men shall be so illuminated thereby, that true and rational liberty shall flourish in every land, and the existence and the very name of slavery be but as a tale that hath been told.

ZAMBA.

CHARLESTON, SOUTH CAROLINA,
February 1846.

CONTENTS.

CHAPTER I.

CHAPTER V.

CHAPTER VI.

CHAPTER VII.

CHAPTER VIII.

THE

LIFE AND ADVENTURES

OF

ZAMBA,

AN AFRICAN NEGRO KING;

AND HIS EXPERIENCE OF

SLAVERY IN SOUTH CAROLINA.

WRITTEN BY HIMSELF.

CORRECTED AND ARRANGED BY

PETER NEILSON.

LONDON:

SMITH, ELDER AND CO., 65, CORNHILL.

1847.

CHAPTER XIV.

CHAPTER XV.

LIFE OF ZAMBA.

CHAPTER I.

Author's Birth and Parentage—Native Village and Royal Palace—
Black King — Court of Justice — Standing Army—Adjacent
Country—Negro Revels—Early Instruction in Religion—Idol-
Worship — Mountain Scenery and Adventure with Baboon—
Negro Priests—Youthful Ideas of a Future State.

To the best of my calculation, I was ushered into
this world of sin and woe in the year 1780. I was
born in a small village situated on the south bank of
the river Congo, about two hundred miles from the
sea, and had the honour to claim as my father, the
chief or king who ruled over this village. His empire
comprised a considerable part of the surrounding
country, and in his own estimation, and that of some
of the neighbouring potentates, he was a personage
of no small importance and dignity.

My father, whose name was Zembola, was a good-
looking and very powerful man, and from his infancy
he had been brought up to despise dangers and
difficulties of every description. To attain the rank
and fame of a great warrior was his sole ambition:

B

far different from many great warriors in more civi-
lised nations, he evinced no desire to extend his
limited dominions.

The village, or metropolis of his kingdom, already
referred to as my birth-place, consisting of about
ninety huts and the king's palace, was built within
a hundred yards of the river, which is here about
half an English mile in breadth. The bank rises
abruptly to about thirty feet above the common level
of the water, and the village is thus placed out of
reach of the highest floods; and a small but beautiful mountain stream issuing from a ravine or glen,
enters the Congo at the east end of the village.

The royal palace towered over all the other buildings, and was in reality a very considerable edifice.
Its form was circular, with an imitation of a dome at
the top, in which hung an old ship's bell that was
rung on all great occasions, either of a mournful or
joyous nature. The interior of the palace was divided
into eighteen or twenty apartments, two of them
especially being furnished in a manner that would
rather astonish an European. The *harem*—you will
no doubt smile, gentle reader, at the use of this term
applied to such an insignificant building, and amongst
such a barbarous people—was furnished with rich
carpets and cushions to recline upon, and embellished
with some very fine mirrors. The audience-chamber
was about twenty feet square, having a floor of
beautiful polished wood, and was furnished with
handsome chairs and tables of foreign manufacture.
The walls were adorned with many fine prints;

amongst them I remember in particular, King George III. on horseback, portraits of several English admirals, and some pictures of sea fights; but above all, a very fine view of London attracted my earliest, and I may say my daily attention.

When a mere boy, I used to stand for hours gazing upon the wilderness of buildings represented in this picture, and oft-times amused myself by endeavouring to count the houses, and even the very windows. My power of calculation, however, could never reach a higher sum than the amount of my own fingers and toes; when this was attained, I had always to " recur to first principles" (as the learned men say, with whom I have since then become acquainted) and reiterate the finger and toe. It may be asked, how did my kingly parent obtain these luxuries? In his intercourse with the slave-traders, which was a considerable part of his avocation. I must not omit to mention the throne, which was elevated somewhat above the other seats and furnished with a canopy of silk and many ornaments of gold and silver. Here, upon special occasions, sat King Zembola, arrayed in garments brought from various nations and climes—mostly old military and naval uniforms, besprinkled with no small quantity of gold and precious stones—and smoking a long tobacco-pipe, with a large crystal bottle of Frank "fire-water" near his elbow. In this state would he, with the utmost coolness and indifference, decide cases of life and death; pronouncing sentence from which there was no appeal. I have seen him,

apparently in a calm and tranquil mood, take the
pipe out of his mouth for a moment, and point with
it to one of a number of poor wretches, whom by
his code of equity he deemed worthy of death, and
order the appointed officers to remove him, and bring
in his head in five minutes! No sooner said than
done; in the required time the bloody and ghastly
head was brought to the foot of the throne, and a
dram of rum, from the hands of royalty itself,
generally rewarded the executioner. I cannot think
that my father was naturally of a cruel disposition,
but education and habit are everything. I question
if any European monarch, enthroned in magnificence
and splendour, and surrounded by his nobles, ever
felt half so self-complacent as my father did with
his score and half of attendants. Like his brother
sovereigns of more extensive empires, my father had
a regular standing army, though, including officers,
amounting only to forty men. But in case of an
invasion of his own kingdom, or his going upon a
foreign expedition, he could muster about one hundred
and fifty fighting men at a day's notice. His " regulars" were all armed with muskets and cutlasses; the
others with spears only, or bows and arrows. With
these latter weapons, however, much execution was
occasionally done.

The village, and about six acres of ground conti-
guous, was surrounded with strong pallisades about
nine feet high; partly as a defence against any sudden
hostile incursion, and partly to exclude wild animals,
which at night were sometimes daring enough to

attempt an attack on the cattle, that were all collected within at sun down. The ground sloped very gradually backwards from the river, until at some miles distance, it rose into considerable mountains. About two hundred yards in the rear of the palace, arose, sheer out of the plain, an insulated hill, in form of a bee-hive, and covered to the summit with trees. It was about five hundred feet high, and a mile or so in circumference. At the very foot of this hill, or rather rock, nature had formed an entrance five or six feet in diameter, and on proceeding a few yards inwards, it opened into an immense cave, capable of containing the whole population of my father's realm. By a little artificial aid, this cave was converted into a stronghold or retreat; and being well secured at the mouth by a gate of iron bars, a small number of men within could defend it for any length of time. In this retreat my father kept his treasures and valuables. These consisted chiefly of European and American goods (of which spirits and tobacco formed a large proportion), that he had received in barter for slaves; for to tell the plain and honest truth, my father was neither more nor less than a flesh and blood merchant. He was also a farmer and grazier to a considerable extent, but only so as to procure mere eatables for his dependants. The whole of his subjects were obliged to labour, when required, upon the royal grounds; but the forty men composing the regular army were, upon the whole, very lazy fellows: little work, save that of cutting throats, firing their enemies' villages, and capturing prisoners, could be got out of them.

In their own line, however, I must own, they were
very expert.

Although my father generally exercised such de-
spotic power over his subjects, there were times when
great familiarity existed between king and people.
On certain holidays, and upon the return of a successful expedition, my father was obliged to allow
great indulgences, especially to his warriors. He
generally submitted to their demands with a good
grace, and revelled and rioted like the best of them.
I remember, at one time, the army having returned,
with King Zembola at their head of course, bringing
fifty prime prisoners, that an uncommon jollification
was resolved upon : nothing less than the audience
chamber for their orgies would please the regulars,
and into this state apartment a barrel of rum and
other requisites for the carousal were brought. My
father mounted his throne, and made a speech (he
did not *read* his speech, as his brother and sister
potentates of Europe do, in general, for alas! poor
man! he was no scholar), and, of course, the said
speech was mightily applauded. If literally trans-
lated into negro's English, it would have run thus :—
" My brave boys, hear me!—I is great, powerful
king! who is bigger than me? Sun look down on me,
call me broder; moon, she do shine. Kiss my hand.
You all brave boys, cause you my men. We go out
fight de Moolah tribe. We all lion,—great roar!
Moolah men, dey all sheep. Poor piccanniny—dey
run away when see King Zembola. We chase dem,—
smite, slay, kill—one. two, tree hundred,—send all to

jumbo (hell). Burn village—take prisoner—fifty, sixty black rascal. Keep dem in' Zembola castle. Buckra captain come soon—buy slave. We get knife, musket, powder, ball, rum—rum. Huzza!— huzza! for King Zembola and his brave boys!"

My father and his regulars (the *militia*, as we may call them, were served outside the palace) continued to drink, and smoke, and feast during the night; and in the morning, when I, at that time a boy of twelve years old, entered the audience chamber, with my mother and two of my sisters, the princesses, there lay, alas! King Zembola on the broad of his back, his hand on the floor, and his feet, or rather his heels, resting on the edge of the throne; he held his crown (a large circlet of pure gold) clenched in his right hand, and a wooden cup half full of rum was grasped in the left. The prime minister lay with his feet across my poor father's stomach, and across him lay a captain of ten. In fact, all ceremony had been banished, and the Frank fire-water had accomplished what hundreds of their fierce and armed foes had failed in doing. My mother, who was a managing woman in her way, had her spouse quietly conveyed to bed, and immediately sent in a score of servants with buckets of water from the Congo, which being dashed profusely in all directions, awoke the whole party.

I have already said that there was a harem in the palace. My father, being a moderate kind of a king, contented himself with five wives. My mother was the only one who had a son, and she was, conse-

quently, in the highest favour.   I had nine half-
sisters; and, as far as I can remember, they were all
very kind to me.   This might partly be owing to a
feeling of selfishness, as they were aware that I
should have much in my power at my father's death.
Independently of this consideration, however, they
were naturally well disposed : indeed (setting aside
scenes of cruelty and blood to which the customs of
the country have habituated them), the women of
Africa in general have much of the milk of human
kindness, and more than one white traveller has con-
firmed this assertion.

I must now recur to circumstances of an earlier
date than those already mentioned.   I trust the indulgent reader will pardon this discursive and irre-
gular manner of writing,—for I have no experience in
book-making.   But I hope that my adherence to real
matters of fact, will atone for any defect of arrangement in this narrative.

Of the first three or four years of my existence, as
is the case, I believe, with most others of the children
of men, I can recollect nothing.   When past the age of
four, I have a clear remembrance of awaking almost
every night after a long sleep, and peeping out of my
little crib or box which was fastened to the side of
the wall, I used to see my mother and her four
queens in companionship with a considerable number
of the domestics, busily engaged in carding and spin-
ning cotton; some few of them also were employed in
weaving.   The cloth was not much above four inches
in breadth, and about the fineness of common English

shirting; and they had the art of dyeing it: generally of a blue colour. Many, many years after, when residing in America, I sometimes saw a few pieces of this cloth brought from Africa; and the sight of it dimmed my eyes with tears when recollection brought back to mind the days of infancy—recalled the midnight manufacturing scenes in my father's house, and the simple, but expressive and affecting songs which invariably accompanied them.

I am certain that I recollect everything of importance which took place after I had attained my sixth year. About that time my mother taught me to bow down every morning before a hideous image which was placed in a particular chamber of the house. This idol was tolerably well carved, and intended, I suppose, to represent the devil: it had a wide mouth stretching from ear to ear, long tusks, and huge goggle eyes, composed of precious stones; and was anything but an attractive object to the infant mind. The words my mother taught me to repeat, were only a few monotonous petitions to this hideous monster to do me no harm—not to burn me, or kill me, or run away with me. It was the worship of fear and terror, not of love. Oh! how far more ennobling and glorious a mode of worship has dawned upon me since—long years ago. But when I think on the millions of my poor benighted relatives and countrymen who are still in the darkness and shadow of death, this, indeed, embitters my recollections; and I can only bow to the dispensations of a great and benevolent Being, who will, finally, vindicate all his ways and all his doings to the sons of men.

For the first five or six years of my life, I was allowed to roll about on the ground or floor, or walk and run as I could, but was never permitted to stray beyond the village enclosure. My father, being somewhat proud of his heir apparent, had me clothed in a red, or yellow garment which was fastened round my waist, and came down to my knees, somewhat like the petticoat worn by Scottish Highlanders; and on my head was a flashy turban adorned with beautiful feathers plucked from the birds of my fatherland, and also with a jewel or two in front. The dress was light and airy, and left me at full liberty to exercise my limbs as instinct dictated.

At the age of eight or nine, I first learned to handle the bow, and soon became expert enough to bring down any small animal at an ordinary distance. I shall never forget my first grand exploit in archery. I have already mentioned that close to the eastern side of the village flowed a beautiful stream which took its rise in the mountains. It ran for many miles through a romantic and lovely glen, which was the retreat of millions of the feathered tribes, and also of numerous quadrupeds. A considerable quantity of gold was found mixed with the sand and gravel of this stream, especially after heavy rains: that is, if any one took the trouble to search for it; for to speak truly, my countrymen were by no means distinguished for industry, when they could avoid working, and the

women had other things to attend to. I often used
to ramble up the bed of this stream, accompanied by
a young companion or two; and sometimes by some
of our own family: for my sisters were very fond of
me. We used to catch in this stream small fish,
which shone like gold and silver; but sometimes we
came across game of rather an unpleasant description, namely, small serpents and other noxious rep-
tiles. We, however, seldom met with any of a size to
alarm us much : the larger craft in general never left
the Congo; but in it were crocodiles of eighteen to
twenty feet in length, and also large sharks. Yet,
although much traffic was carried on upon the water,
and especially on the great river as it was called,
there were seldom any lives lost.

One day, accompanied by my sister Lemba, who
at that time was about thirteen, while my age was
eleven, with my bow and arrows in hand, I went to
the stream, determined upon an excursion of some
distance along its course. There was a splendid
waterfall about half a mile up the glen, beyond
which we had been previously warned by our parents
not to wander. A prohibition of this kind, amongst
almost every race of mankind, generally serves as a
stimulus to young people to see *what is round the
corner*, as it were ; and so it was with Lemba and I:
with gay and light hearts we proceeded on and on,
although surmounting the rocky precipice, over which
was the waterfall, was a work of some difficulty.
When we reached the summit, young as we were,
we could not help lifting up our hands in admiration

of the grandeur and magnificence of the scene here presented to our view. The river was a stream which an ordinary man could step across when it was not swelled by the rains; but in the lapse of ages it had worn out a most fantastic and curious channel for itself through the solid rock: at every few yards it had made an excavation, like a large cauldron, and these cavities were evidently connected by unseen apertures, causing the water to boil, and toss, and foam unceasingly. Some of these pools, again, were tolerably calm, and in them we could see the glittering fish sporting by hundreds in the element, which was literally pure as crystal. The banks of the stream were here only about ten feet apart, and rose abruptly to at least a hundred feet in height; the light of day appearing at top as if shining through a narrow chink, and rendering every thing below only half visible, in a kind of twilight. Shrubs and bushes, of a thousand varieties, sprang from the sides, and upon these sported birds, monkeys, squirrels, and other children of the forest, who almost deafened us with their incessant and uncouth cries: they seemed unanimously to agree that Lemba and I were intruders on their sequestered domains.

We continued, however, to advance, amid the uproar, for a few hundred yards, and could perceive from the increasing light that the ravine was widening. At last we sat down upon a ledge of rock, and my sister, from a small basket which she had carried from home, took out something for us to eat. While we were satisfying our hunger, a pretty large stone fell at our feet, and instantly a most hideous yell arose, which was heard above all the other noises; when upon looking up we perceived seated on the corner of a rock a huge blue-faced baboon, grinning at and threatening us in a most horrible manner.

Poor Lemba fell a trembling, but presently recovering herself she snatched hold of my hand, and said, " Zamba! Zamba! come, let us go home as quietly as possible. Keep your bow in readiness, but do not attempt to run. I will be cunning with baboon, else it may be bad for us."

She instantly took a bit of what we were eating, and laid it upon the stone, and then we cautiously commenced our retreat. On looking back we could perceive the ugly fellow spring at one bound to the place we had left.

We continued retreating as quickly as possible, always leaving a little of our food in the way; this delayed the enemy, but when just at the brink of the precipice we had to lay down our last morsel. The baboon seemed determined not to lose sight of us, and chattered most furiously as we were sliding down the precipice at rather a quicker rate than we had climbed up. ' We reached the bottom in safety, but looking up we saw our enemy preparing to descend. Although very much frightened, I adjusted my arrow with tolerable steadiness, and let fly; it was well aimed, I believe, but a small branch of a tree intervened, into which the arrow stuck. The animal seemed to understand that the arrow was sent

with no friendly purpose, and attempted to pull it
out of the branch; as he was leaning over for the
purpose, and just at the critical moment, I sent
another, which completely transfixed our foe, who
came tumbling to the ground with a hideous yell.
Lemba and I did not stop to examine the wound, but
made the best of our way home; and then what a
tale of horror and interest we had to tell. My father,
although displeased at our wandering beyond limits,
clapped me on the shoulder, and said, " Now, Zamba,
you are a man; I shall soon take you on my expeditions, and you shall have a musket to shoot men with
instead of monkeys." He then sent two of his regulars to bring the dead baboon, and, after it had been
skinned, my father had it properly stuffed, and
placed in such a part of the palace as would do
honour to young Prince Zamba's courage and Lemba's prudence. The fact is, that such an animal
would have been a match for a stout man, if without his weapons; and on hearing the remarks of my
father's dependants, who, of course, all paid court to
the heir apparent, I swelled with pride like a
turkey-cock.

Those among my readers who feel interested in
this narrative, may, perhaps, be inclined to ask,
" Were you receiving any proper education all this
time? Had you a teacher? Had you any ideas
beyond the things visible around? Did you know
anything of a future state?" To such questions my
reply is, that I had no teacher of letters; and as for
matters of religion, our ideas were extremely dull and

erroneous. There were two priests in my father's dominions; but the fact is they were mere jugglers: not only ignorant, but licentious. They occasionally visited every house, muttering some gibberish, and performing many antics to astonish the women, and never failed to collect a pretty good revenue. On certain days of each year they came forth in a sort of disguise, wearing masks, and every soul they encountered was obliged to provide a present, get it where and how he might; and there was a particular day in the year when they came forth masked, and the first person they met had either to pay a very heavy ransom, or be slain as a sacrifice. In some few instances, which I well remember, the sacrifice was enforced in a manner too horrible to relate; and this merely to keep up the authority of these wretched impostors.

My father, in his intercourse with the white men who came to trade with him, had picked up some confused ideas of another world and of futurity; but he troubled himself very little about the matter. And are there not millions in civilized Europe, enjoying every opportunity of religious instruction, who are just as indifferent to the fate of their immortal souls? When I was even a boy some very strange ideas of time and space entered my mind. I used sometimes in the evening to lie down upon the ground, and gaze for an hour or two upon the glittering stars with feelings of indescribable delight. The sun was too dazzling and splendid to gaze much upon; but the moon—the mild and gentle moon, and the innumerable clusters of beautiful stars, fascinated my sight, and filled my mind with wonder. For what they were made, how they were made, and of what they were made, altogether puzzled my imagination. I sometimes, however, reasoned thus : Suppose I were carried this moment to yonder light star, what then should I see? More stars I should think. And what then? More again—still more and more; and then all will be darkness and nothing. But what then would be beyond that darkness? This was the puzzle. In the same way I reasoned regarding time. After father die, I shall be king—then I have son, he king—he have son again, more king—more son, more king. And what then? No end can I see. World burn up—all things end. But *how* end ?—*something* must be. I could come to no definite or satisfactory conclusion; yet I think that such thoughts prove that Divine Providence, the Light of Nature, or whatever it may be called, influenced me to a certain degree, even in wild and dark Africa.

CHAPTER II.

Trading in Slaves, &c.—African Cannibalism—Romantic Scenery—
Lion Hunting—Singular Waterfall—Gooloo Bamba, a Negro
King—Zamba's danger.

I HAVE said that my father had much intercourse
with white men. His principal business, indeed, was
to procure cargoes of living flesh and blood, to be
transported to some far land towards the setting sun.
The slave ships, which came to this part of Africa,
generally anchored a few miles within the mouth of
the Congo, as there they lay secure from the everlasting surf which rolls all along the western coast.
Sometimes my father carried down his people, as he
called them, to the slavers in large canoes ; but not
unfrequently the white captain, with a crew of ten or
twelve men, came up to my father's residence. It
was, in fact, a convenient depôt for trading in other
matters. A white man was, consequently, no strange
sight to me, even from earliest infancy. There was
an American, Captain Winton, who traded for many
years with my father. It was he who had brought all
the fine furniture for the palace, and amongst other

C

toys he brought a large violin for me; but, as we had no instructor, the sounds which my father, myself, or any of his people elicited from it, would by no means have set the stones a-dancing. On one occasion, however, when I had carried the violin into the woods, it providentially had the effect of setting a whole troop of hyenas to their heels: to my great relief and amazement. At last this Captain Winton brought a small barrel-organ, which could play eight tunes; and, having instructed us how to change the tunes, it became a constant treat to prince and peasant: I really think that for six months after we received it, it was not quiet for six minutes. Like all other things, however, it fell into disuse, and was soon set aside as an incumbrance. I must confess, by the way, that my countrymen in general, though fond of music, are extremely capricious and volatile in their disposition. To proceed. This Captain Winton and his men were sometimes inmates of the palace for eight or ten days at a time, therefore I soon learned to pick up many English words, and could soon bear part in a conversation in that language. My father entertained the white men very hospitably, and presents were continually being exchanged. I may mention, however, as an instance of the way this traffic went on, that Captain Winton received two fine slaves for the barrel-organ.

To procure cargoes of slaves, my father went upon an expedition every now and then with his regulars; that is, he went to a distant part of the country, and found ways and means to pick a quarrel with some less powerful tribe, which generally ended by the weaker tribe giving up a number of slaves as ransom; or a fight took place, and the strongest helped themselves. To do my father justice, however, he made it a rule never to quarrel with his *next* neighbours; he rather kept on terms with them, and, consequently, they served as a kind of rampart or wall to guard him against the incursions of others. Besides the slaves which he obtained in his warlike expeditions, he procured many more by *fair* trade: if the term may be applied in such a case. He often sailed up the Congo with a supply of English or American goods, and by bartering these to petty kings, several hundreds of miles up the country, he never failed to come back with a full cargo, at reasonable prices. He also procured gold dust, ivory, and other valuable commodities, in the same way. His kingly office was, in fact, no sinecure; for to keep up such an establishment as my father did required considerable exertion and prudence. I may mention here, that after I was in America I heard it frequently asserted by white men that my countrymen were cannibals. From my own experience I should have said that this was very incorrect, but my father told me that in one of his journeys, about four hundred miles further up the river than his own kingdom, he had seen exposed for sale publicly in the market of a town, the name of which I forget, human limbs regularly cut up; and this I must not gainsay, as he could have no interest in making a false statement to me.

My father proved as good as his word in en-
trusting me with a gun, and about half a year after
the baboon exploit he procured me a short rifle, with
which I practised for an hour or two every day, and
in a month or two handled it pretty well. In my
own imagination I considered myself now a match
for a score of baboons or hyenas, or even for a lion of
moderate size; and it was not long before my skill
was put to the test. My father had appointed a
regular hunting-match to take place, as several
depredations had been committed upon his flocks not
far from the village. About two hundred men were
mustered on the occasion, and at my own urgent
request I was allowed to accompany them. My
father was really a very daring fellow, and as chief
always considered it his duty to be foremost in
danger. He, however, took good care to be well
armed at all points. He had a fine double-barrelled
rifle, a short cutlass by his side, a pair of pistols
stuck in his belt, and an attendant close by him,
carrying, for his master's use, a very strong spear,
the head of which, about fifteen inches in length,
was made of the finest steel, pointed, and double-
edged. The shaft was about six feet long, made of
lance-wood, and nearly as thick as a man's arm,
so that in close encounter with any very large animal
there would be no risk of its breaking. Having all
assembled before daybreak at the palace, a dram of
rum was served out to every man, and, each being
supplied with provisions for two days, forth they
went. When we had proceeded about two miles the

sun arose, and by the time we had gained a certain
point where the river Congo took a slight bend, one
of the finest views, I believe, in Africa opened on our
sight. Great part of the country before us was open,
interspersed with splendid natural clumps of the teak
tree, while here and there orange and palm trees
adorned the scene; fields of Guinea corn, eighteen
or twenty feet in height, waved in the morning breeze,
the beautiful broad-leaved Indian corn, or maize,
spread its waving blades in the air, and then a field
of cotton might be seen. Not far distant lay our
village, and near it were herds of cattle and goats,
and even the labourers at work in the fields might
be discerned. I forgot the hunt for a few minutes
in admiring this lovely scene ; and even now, when
I recur to that morning, after the lapse of nearly
half a century, I cannot help inwardly ejaculating,
" When, oh ! when, will poor benighted, yet beautiful Africa, be brought completely and wholly under the mild and glorious influence of Christian
civilization?"

My attention was soon drawn from the enchanting
scenery around me, by the incessant blowing of
horns and yelling of dogs, intermingled with the
incipient growling of wild beasts. Scores of hyenas
and other wild animals of the smaller kind, fled
before us, and occasionally one was shot down: I
cannot say how many were killed that day. We
did not fall in with any formidable beast till towards
mid-day, when a tremendous lion was started.
Instantly our whole troop was on the alert, and

some who had been very forward at first, now exhibited symptoms of disinclination to be in the front.
My father, however, seemed quite in his element,
and told me to keep close to him, but a little behind.
When I got a view of the lion, which was the
first I had seen, I really felt very strange: it was
quite a different looking creature from the baboon.
The beast retired very slowly, frequently stopping
and looking round, lashing its sides with its tail,
and uttering short low growls, which to my boyish
imagination, appeared actually to shake the earth.
It had been repeatedly fired at, but as yet evidently
without serious effect, and at last it was brought to
a stand in a small ravine, through which there was
no egress. When the lion discovered its situation,
it turned full round, and glared with eyes of fire
on its pursuers, still lashing its sides; and now
and then as some over-venturesome dog rushed forward, striking its assailant to the ground with its
paw, as easily as a man could crush an egg-shell
with his foot. My father with his attendant, soon
approached within thirty or forty yards; he levelled
his rifle with the utmost coolness, telling me in a
suppressed voice to fall back, and then fired. The
lion uttered a sharp roar and shook itself, but still
stood its ground. Again my father fired, and then
the animal advanced several yards. Its aspect was
terribly grand: its mane which was long enough to
reach the ground, stood nearly erect like an immense
ruff around its neck, and stretching out its fore-feet,
it crouched behind considerably; still keeping its

glaring eyes fixed on its foe. My father coolly reached
out his hand to his attendant and received his spear,
and then advanced to within ten yards of the beast,
holding his weapon in readiness. At this instant
the attitudes of the man and the lion would have
made a magnificent picture. My father after a moment's pause, knelt on one knee, holding the butt
of his spear firmly to the ground, with the point
sloping towards the lion; he then uttered a loud and
peculiar kind of cry, when the animal answering
with a tremendous roar made a spring; my father
still holding up the spear, leapt on one side with
great agility, and the huge monster was completely
transfixed. It rolled and twisted about in every
direction, until some of the hunters rushed in and
despatched him. Had my father not leapt aside at
the instant, he would probably have received some
deadly wounds from the struggling beast; but he was
experienced in such encounters. He told me, after we
came home, that having failed in both his last shots, he
was determined to venture an attack upon the lion
with his spear. His men looked upon him as in-
vincible; and he could not think of retreating and
leaving one of his subjects to conquer what had
baffled himself. My father now ordered all hands
to halt, and a general refreshment to be given. The
lion was speedily stripped of its skin, and it was
found to measure from the nose to the rump about
eight English feet; the tail being three or four feet
in addition. There was not a man present who could
with both hands clasp the leg round above the fore

knee-joint: some idea may thus be formed of its enormous size.

After resting for about a couple of hours, the heat being intense, every one was again on his feet, for it was strongly suspected, by the same experienced hunters, from certain marks and indications which had been seen, that the lion's partner could not be far off. And so it turned out; for the lioness was started within a mile of the spot where her royal spouse fell, and she made off with all speed for the higher grounds. It was near sun-down when we saw her enter a ravine, and this being a well known locality, a general shout was given; as from this retreat she had no means of escape. The ravine, from which a small stream issued, was not above four feet wide: in some parts two men could hardly pass each other, and the rocks on each side rose at least a hundred feet perpendicularly. About a hundred yards from the entrance, the narrow chasm opened into an immense plain, as level and smooth as a cultivated field, about eight or ten acres in extent, and surrounded on all sides by precipitous cliffs, upwards of two hundred feet in height, clothed to the top with trees and shrubs of every description. At the farther end a beautiful spout of water came sheer over the precipice (the edge of which projected), and fell into a basin at least thirty feet from the bottom of the rock; appearing like a stream of molten silver as the sun shone upon it, and when the wind blew with any violence, it swayed to and fro like a solid band of metal. It was designated by a term in the African tongue, signifying the " crystal chain."

Our whole troop having entered this retreat, the lioness was soon discovered crouching behind a rock, and growling terribly. My father, having already done his part sufficiently for one day, allowed all who chose to have a shot at the poor beast, and I suppose about fifty balls were sent into her. Orders were soon given to encamp for the night. In this enclosed space I believe ten thousand men might have found ample accommodation. Timber in large quantities was soon collected, and several immense fires were kindled; and as a considerable number of the animals which had been killed during the day were of a palatable description, and other provisions had been brought out, a hearty supper was partaken of by all. My father being in a particularly good humour, gave orders that every man should receive a small measure of spirts—enough to enliven, but not to intoxicate.

I may here take occasion to remark, that King Zembola was upon the whole rather a temperate man, considering his habits, his avocations, and his opportunities. Several of his neighbouring potentates, who could only maintain a body-guard of six or eight men, did nothing day after day but sit beneath the shade of a tree with their pipes in their mouths, and a keg of rum beside them, and were assisted in the evening to their dormitory in a state of oblivion. So long as their funds lasted they " kept the war up," as the saying is; and there was

one merry fellow, but an awful drunkard, named
Gooloo Bambo, who again and again pawned his ornaments, and even one of his wives, to my father for a
keg of rum. These, however, as soon as he could
raise the means otherwise were honourably redeemed.
Who could have thought that the civilized art of
pawnbroking had been carried on in heathen Africa!

This King Gooloo was a very eccentric fellow in
some of his notions, particularly in regard to dress.
At one period he had procured from a slave-trader
a very beautiful scarlet long-tailed coat, covered with
buttons and gold lace, which he wore close buttoned
to the chin, but without vest, pantaloons, or even a
shirt; on his head he stuck a naval officer's cocked
hat, and thrust his feet into a pair of good English
top-boots, but as to a shirt, he scorned such an
effeminate garment. My father earnestly advised
him to wear a shirt at least, if he dispensed with
unmentionables. "No, no," said he; "shirt made
for Buckra man—shirt like woman petticoat. King
Gooloo, brave warrior—have no shirt." I saw him
one day, after he had generously made the whole of
his staff-officers and male attendants dead drunk,
strutting in the dress I have described, with a musket
over his shoulder, and doing duty as sentry at his
own palace door, muttering to himself occasionally,—
"King Gooloo—big fellow—great prince; wonder
what English people say 'bout me — what King
George think; go see him some day. What 'Merican
people say of me. Oh, Gomo! Gomo! I 'stonish
them some day." He would then go over to the

rum-keg, and very gravely drink his own health. I am by no means exaggerating in regard to King Gooloo; and perhaps, if the curtain were withdrawn, his brother monarchs in more enlightened parts of the earth might also exhibit a few traits of eccentricity.

To return to our encampment. Night set in immediately after supper, but some of the troop were disposed for sleep. War-dances, accompanied by frightful yells, were commenced, and continued till about midnight. Had any European traveller arrived that evening at the edge of the precipice above us, the scene presented to his view must have been very striking. The night was particularly dark, which rendered the light cast by the huge fires more glaring; and the dark shadows and lurid reflections cast by every object around appeared to me altogether magnificent. Nothing seemed more fantastic than the slender stream of water rushing through the air: it gleamed and flashed in the flickering light like a cataract of diamonds. The wild beasts, which held dominion in this quarter, being disturbed, kept up an incessant howling and chattering the whole night: hyenas, baboons, monkeys, and many other animals, joined their discordant notes to the screaming of numberless tribes of the parrot kind; and small flocks of the large black vulture, so common in this part of Africa, flitted about from tree to tree and from rock to rock, seeming, to my boyish imagination, hordes of evil spirits in quest of a resting-place, or watching for an opportunity of pouncing upon our

troop, as at last they lay outstretched in sleep. Long
ere daybreak many of the party were astir, replenish-
ing the fires, taking a morning smoke, or preparing
for breakfast. This meal was no sooner despatched
than we again started in search of game. I had the
satisfaction of bringing down two hyenas and an
antelope. Besides these, only a few small animals
were killed by the rest of the party. By the afternoon, our village was again in sight.

The death of the pair of lions relieved our flocks from
all disturbance for a long time afterwards, and the adventures of this hunting expedition served to wile away
many a long evening. I felt so much pleased with the
result of this hunt, that I determined to apply myself
regularly to the use of the gun, and, if possible, rival
my father in his prowess. Accordingly, I practised at
a mark every day, and frequently made short excursions, always bringing in a greater or less quantity of
game. By the time I had attained my thirteenth year,
I could hit an egg, suspended to the end of a cane at
the distance of a hundred yards, with a single ball; and
having performed this feat several times before my
father, he allowed me, in company with an attendant
or two, to take an excursion to any distance not
exceeding two days' journey. I made free use of this
license, and encountered many adventures and mishaps ere I reached my fifteenth year; but I shall only
trouble the reader with an anecdote or two.

When I was about fourteen, having a good consti-
tution, and being well taken care of in regard to food,
&c., I had become, by free exercise, very stout and

active for my age, and indeed was a match in strength
and agility for many men arrived at maturity. I one
day went forth, accompanied by two clever servants
named Pouldamah and Bollah—lads who would
not, I was confident, flinch at any danger—and
having shot several hyenas, I got so eager in
the sport that nothing would serve me but a lion
encounter, if such could be obtained. I offered a
handsome reward to the man who would first start
one; and having stretched far into the wildest part of
the forest, our ears were at last assailed by the deep
and low growl of one of the forest kings. Our dogs
soon led us into a hollow, where we perceived a large-
sized lion regaling himself on the new-slain carcass
of a wild goat. At sight of us, he merely turned
round for an instant, and then proceeded with his
meal, munching and growling alternately like a dog
over a bone. Without a moment's hesitation, I fired,
and hit him on one of the ears. This only irritated
him; and before my companions could bring their
pieces to a bearing, the huge beast was down upon
us with a tremendous roar; and in turning tail,
which I naturally did, I fell over a stone and lay
prostrate on my face. My companions also had
taken to their heels on the instant; but, partly
through faithfulness to me and their own natural
courage, and partly perhaps through fear of my
father's anger — which would have been fatal to
them, had anything happened to me—they rallied
and stood firm for a moment. The lion coming up
with me, laid one of his paws on my back, and put-

ting his nose close to me, began to growl and snuff. The weight of his paw was tremendous, and even painful; but, as I had been warned by old hunters of the habits and ways of the lion tribe, I lay dead still, and held in my breath until almost suffocated. When just about to give in for want of breath, I heard two sharp cracks, and in a moment my huge enemy was rolling on the ground. I arose " pretty smartly," as the Americans say, and rushed to my two faithful friends, who clasped me with delight, and even cried for joy. In the mean time, the animal continued to roll and tumble about in his death agonies, and had we not kept at a respectful distance until he was quite spent, we should probably have paid dearly for our temerity. After taking his dimensions, which we found little inferior to the one my father had so daringly encountered, we took away his skin as a trophy.

And now, it may be inquired, how it happened that I, who was so expert a shot as to hit an egg at a hundred yards distance, did not mortally wound my enemy at first? The truth is, that I felt not quite so steady in my aim as the son of a brave chief ought to have done; and, farther, I can assure my readers that it is one thing to aim at an egg placed upon an inanimate object, and another to aim at the said egg placed on the forehead of a living and fierce lion.

I might mention many other encounters that I had with wild animals as I increased in years; but not to become tiresome on one subject, shall close my hunting adventures with another anecdote. One

day, I went forth with about a dozen of my father's
regulars, and after killing some small game, we fell
in with a flock of antelopes, of which we were eagerly
in pursuit through a kind of open country or prairie,
where the grass and weeds grew two or three feet
high. I had taken a hasty leap over a small rut,
and, alighting on something soft and slippery, fell
prostrate; ere I could recover myself, I felt something twist round my body, and roll me over and
over. In a moment it occurred to me that I was
within the folds of a serpent. I was squeezed so
tightly, that I had only time to give one loud scream
for assistance, and instinctively raise my arms upwards in the endeavour to defend my head and face ;
being aware, from what I had heard from others,
that the serpent would endeavour to make a twist
round my neck. I could hear the monster hissing
and playing its head round my face, but could not
see: either through pain or horror at my situation.
I gradually felt my ribs bending beneath its cruel
gripe, and imagined that all was over with me,
when to my inexpressible relief, I heard the voices
of my friends; one of whom, with his cutlass, at
one blow severed the monster's head from its body.
It still, however, held me firm in its gripe, but
speedily two or three of my faithful attendants threw
themselves on the tail part of the animal, whilst
another cut about two feet off from its extremity.
Instantly I felt relieved, but was quite unable to
stand or speak. Fortunately water was at hand, and
I soon came to myself, though now quite unconcerned

about pursuing antelopes or any other game—for that day, at least. The stench which proceeded either from the breath of the serpent, or from its fluids when cut asunder, was suffocating ; and when relieved from its folds, I was covered with blood and slime. As near as we could make out its dimensions, the serpent was about sixteen feet in length, and at the thickest part it was about the size of the leg of a stout man. It was a boa constrictor, and its bite was not poisonous ; although it left a mark or two on one of my arms which did not wear off for some years. For many days afterwards, I shuddered at the sight, or even at the mention, of a snake of any description ; and for a long while after, I occasionally screamed out in my dreams ; nor have I altogether got quit of my horror even at this day. While I lay prostrate beneath the paw of the lion, as before mentioned, I felt very uncomfortable—exceedingly so, indeed ; but that was nothing to be compared to what I endured whilst held in the folds of the serpent : the feeling was horrible—truly horrible !

CHAPTER III.

Arrival of American Captain—Visit to his ship—Trading expedition
—King Darroola's village—Festivities—Darroola's treachery and
skirmish—Zembola vows vengeance.

I SHALL now advert to other occurrences than hunting. My father made regular excursions with his
men, and occasionally to a considerable distance,
either for the purpose of quarrelling with some other
tribe, and helping himself to what fortune threw in
his way, or for the more laudable purpose of trading
with other chiefs. He refused, however, upon all
occasions to let me join him, saying that it was too
much to risk both king and prince at one time. He
traded with various slave captains, both British and
American ; but his chief customer was Captain
Winton, who generally came every year, sometimes
oftener. He brought many curiosities to my father
to adorn his palace. We had even a very handsome
London-made eight-day clock, various articles of
crystal, crockery, and hardware, and even some
elegant silver plate, and—what might be deemed
very unnecessary for such ignoramuses as we all

D

were—many handsome printed books with fine plates. My father understood that all civilized princes had fine libraries, and he wished not to be behind any of them. I often used to turn over and over the leaves of these volumes, and would get Captain Winton, when he was not engaged in business, to explain their nature to me; and he would occasionally read a story out of one of them. Sometimes their contents related to our own Africa, describing matters so naturally and truly, that to all of us it seemed quite incomprehensible, and indeed supernatural, that these books should talk better than our wisest men. I felt so much interested by what I heard read, and so eager to know more, that I absolutely bothered Captain Winton to give me some lessons in reading; and to him I owe the rudiments of my education. In his different visits, he enabled me completely to master the English alphabet, and even to read, in a manner, words of one syllable. For my instruction, he brought me an English primer, and I proved a very industrious scholar.

I must be permitted to say, that nature had certainly formed me in a more intellectual and thoughtful mould than the most of my countrymen; and I could not shut my eyes to the fact that, in knowledge, we were far, far behind the strangers who visited us. The various manufactures they brought us was another proof that we were but as infants in comparison to the whites. The more I thought upon the matter, the stronger became my desire to know more of the world and of mankind than what I could

acquire in Africa; and I hinted this my desire to
Captain Winton. But when my father learned that
I had a wish to see foreign nations, he was quite
indignant, and forbade me again to mention the subject. This prohibition, however, like many others to
young minds, had merely the effect of setting me
brooding on the matter, and contriving how to attain
my object.

Captain Winton was a considerable favourite with
the female part of our household. He never forgot
to bring a few trinkets for them,—most of them,
doubtless, of brass well gilded,—and in return he
was sure to obtain real bullion in one shape or other.
The women were very eager to procure small silver
coins, with which they made very pretty necklaces
and bracelets, stringing a coin and an amber or coral
bead alternately. On gala days, my sisters carried
about in this way, on their heads, necks, and arms,
as much small change as an extensive retail shop
would require.

I had attained the age of sixteen, when Captain
Winton, having arrived, I earnestly requested of
my father that he would permit me to go down
the river when the captain went, and see his ship
at the same time. At length he consented, saying that he had a lot of slaves to take down to the
vessel, and that we would all go together. Having
arranged matters, and shipped his slaves, amounting
to fifty-two, in two large canoes, he and I, with twelve
of the regulars, embarked in another, and the captain
accompanied us with his boat, in which were eight

men. In two days, we arrived at the anchoring-ground, which was four miles within the bar that stretched across the mouth of the Congo.

On approaching this spot, where lay four other slave-ships, I was struck with wonder and amazement at the beautiful appearance and gigantic size of these ships, never having before seen any vessel larger than our canoes. After reaching the deck of Captain Winton's ship, the *Triton*, I could hardly believe but that all I saw was enchantment. This vessel carried twelve guns; and, in honour of our visit, Captain Winton ordered a salute of five guns to be fired. I was, of course, well enough acquainted with the explosion of small arms, but had never seen a cannon fired; and as I had no warning of what was about to take place either from my father or the captain (who, no doubt, wished to try my mettle), on the first gun being discharged, I leaped a considerable height from the deck, and looked round at my father perfectly thunderstruck. Indeed, I imagined it actually was thunder, and it was some time before I could recover my composure. When an explanation took place, however, it more surely convinced me of the wonderful power and knowledge possessed by white men.

On being taken down to the cabin, I was shown some articles that appeared to me very curious; amongst others, two very large globes, the nature of which the captain explained. My father laughed outright when he was told that this earth was round, and said,—" Oh, captain, you are making fool of black men." Several maps were also explained to us, and even the nature of eclipses was endeavoured to be illustrated to us by means of some diagrams; but Captain Winton's endeavours were often fruitless, as it was impossible for him to supply us with comprehension. Yet, although I could not understand all he said to us, I was convinced, from other circumstances, that the white man must be in the right, however mysterious it then appeared to me.

After thinking for some time, I inquired of the captain if he knew who made the world, and the sun and moon, and all other visible things. He answered, that one great and invisible Being had made all things, and that the idols we Africans worshipped were merely things invented by the imagination and ignorance of men. He also said that God in former times had sent visible angels from heaven to instruct and direct men in what was right, but that, through the wickedness of mankind, God had been displeased, and no more held visible intercourse with men. Yet that God in his mercy sent his Son, who had come into this world about two thousand years ago, and gave men good instructions and advice; and at last, because he was superior in goodness to any being who had ever appeared on this earth, he was slain by wicked men; but in three days he rose from his grave, and soon afterwards ascended up into heaven, in the presence of many witnesses. All who believed in this Son of God, and repented of their evil works, Captain Winton told me, would after their death be taken to heaven, where they would for ever be happy. All this, although in a great measure

incomprehensible to me at the time, made a deep
impression on my mind; and when I compared such
things to the confused nonsense told to us by our
itinerant priests, I longed from my heart to know
something more of this Son of God. May I ask,
now, if such feelings were not infused into my heart
by the Holy Spirit of God, at that time, and not
merely in consequence of a few sentences spoken by
a slave captain? If not from this cause, from
whence did they arise? I was now determined more
and more, although I kept my thoughts to myself,
that as soon as it was in my power I would make a
voyage to the white man's country.

Captain Winton then showed us the hold of the
ship, and in this there were already stowed, including
my father's cargo, nearly three hundred slaves; they
were mostly in fetters or shackles, and seemed otherwise very uncomfortable. Captain Winton told us
that if he did not thus confine them, they would, when
at sea, come on deck, and make such a confusion in
the ship, that the men would be unable to do their
work. This seemed plausible enough. I then asked
him what would become of the slaves when he
arrived in America. " Oh!" said he, laughing,
" the women will all get white husbands, and will
have little to do but dress and go about: they will
be dressed, Prince Zamba, much better than your
mother and your sisters; and as for the men,
they will be taught to work at various trades, and
will be well fed and clothed, and be far better
off than in Africa." I swallowed all this implicitly,

and thought that in reality they would be better off than if kept by my father and other chiefs as prisoners, in which situation they had no security for their lives for one hour. Captain Winton, however, did not tell me all the facts of the case. I learned them afterwards by my own bitter experience.

We stopped on board the ship all night, and next day my father received payment for his lot of slaves. At this time a stout male slave was valued, on an average, at from thirty to forty dollars, women from five to ten dollars less, and children in proportion. But the purchase was all paid in barter. A piece of common Irish linen was taken at from twenty-five to thirty-five dollars. A musket and bayonet, which in Birmingham probably cost thirty shillings, brought twenty dollars; and gunpowder was priced at a dollar per pound weight. My father, however, would sometimes insist upon having a hundred or two of specie dollars, and seemed quite acquainted with their relative value to manufactured goods. Having arranged all with Captain Winton, we embarked in our canoes, and ere we were a mile on our way up the river, I had the pleasure to see one of the slave vessels under weigh, with a fine breeze; it was truly a marvellous spectacle to me. As we had three canoes in charge, with few hands, it was five days before we reached home.

About seven months after this excursion, my father told me he would take me upon a trading expedition; and farther promised that hereafter he would also take me in his war expeditions,—in fact that we should always keep together and take our chance.   He made me promise solemnly, that, in case anything befell him, I would endeavour to walk in his footsteps, and do all things just as he had done.   I did so; but I must confess, with secret misgivings, as I had quite different ideas in my head.   The expedition he was now bent on, he told me, was to pay a visit and trade with a brother king, named Darroola, of the Kormantu tribe, who resided about two hundred miles from our place, up the Congo.   This Darroola, he said, was a very strange fellow, and it required great caution and courage to deal with him to advantage.   However, I should soon be able to judge for myself.   We had three of our largest canoes put in order, each of which would carry from forty to fifty men; the one in which my father himself embarked had a sort of cabin amid ships, and was furnished with an awning and other conveniences.   Our merchandise—consisting chiefly of Irish linen, red flannel, flashy English printed cotton, and some hardware, with five barrels containing about a hundred gallons of rum, and provisions for the voyage—was put on board the canoes, and we were accompanied by thirty of our best men well armed.

After a passage of six days, mostly accomplished by dint of paddling, we came to King Darroola's landing-place, where we left the vessels in charge of five of the men, and then in formal order proceeded to the village, which made a handsome appearance at about a mile distant.   We were soon descried,

and King Darroola, at the head of twenty or thirty
men, came marching down to meet us. The two
chiefs appeared delighted to see each other; and I
was regularly introduced. King Darroola's appearance was very striking and commanding, but there
was something particularly savage in his smile, and
his eyes, which were extraordinarily large, looked
horribly malignant. He was dressed in red flannel
breeches, with large knee-buckles—his bare legs
showing above a pair of half boots; a blue naval
uniform coat, with large gold epaulettes; and a red
and blue striped night-cap.

As we neared the village, which was surrounded
with pallisades, some of his men commenced blowing
trumpets, and huzzaing with all their might. On
entering the gate, the most conspicuous building was
the palace, of course, which was really a very decent
looking building, of two stories in height. I could,
as we drew near to the palace gate, perceive several
ladies at the upper windows, one of whom beat
upon a drum, and another rattled a tambourine vigorously in honour of our approach. The pallisades
which surrounded the palace on all sides presented
a ghastly, and to me an appalling sight. At the
distance of about every three feet, a human head was
stuck on the end of a small pole; some of them
appeared quite fresh, others were in various stages
of putrefaction. I noticed that the pallisade at one
side of the palace was destitute of these horrible
trophies: the cause of this was soon explained.
Just as my father was entering the gate, he stepped

into a small pool of fresh blood, when, without
appearing in the least astonished, he turned round
to his brother king, and with a half serious, half
comical look, said,—" What! King Darroola, still
keeping up the old amusement? You are too
extravagant, sir. I am sure you always find me
ready enough to bargain for your prisoners or
your criminals. What have you been about this
morning?"—" Ah," answered Darroola, " you know,
King Zembola, that I can afford more heads than
you. It is only for pocket-money I deal with you.
I must have my palace adorned like a true king. I
have about fifty blank spaces to fill up yet, and have
only furnished three this morning." He then explained that he had made it a rule, every new moon,
to fill up at least three vacancies on the pallisades,
until they should be furnished all round with heads.
One of these he had taken this day, he added,
belonged to one of his wives, of whom he was jealous; another was the head of a slave, who had
broken by accident a fine crystal bottle; and the
third, that of a prisoner who was rather sickly, and
who would not, he believed, have brought ten dollars
at all events. He coolly pointed out the three heads,
which had been just stuck up in their places, and
were still dripping with gore. My father only
said, " Sir—sir, you are very extravagant." But
the impression made upon my feelings was such
that I could not help shuddering at the hideous
spectacle; which Darroola perceiving, he clapped me
on the shoulder, and said, " Ah, boy—boy, you

have not seen the world, I perceive." I inwardly hoped that I should soon be far from a country of such horrors, and again reverted in my own mind to what Captain Winton had told me regarding the manner in which white men lived.

On entering the interior of the palace, I observed that, although well furnished for an African prince, it had not the tasteful arrangement or handsome ornaments of my father's house; but a great many spoils of the chase lay scattered about, and the walls in every direction were adorned with implements of war. The two chiefs now sat down at a table, and, excepting myself, all others were ordered out. They then commenced to talk of business; bottles of spirits and other refreshments were produced, and after a few cups were drunk, Darroola inquired how much rum his brother had brought with him. To this and other questions, my father answered in an evasive manner, inquiring in return how many and what kind of prisoners Darroola had on hand; who, like a true merchant, also evaded the question: in fact, the two for a long time, like abler tacticians in more civilized countries, appeared to be striving to get the weather-gauge of each other. At length they came to some kind of terms, and I found, by the prices agreed upon for the various articles to be given for fifty-five slaves, that my father drove a very profitable trade: he gained cent. per cent. at least on every article, and as much upon the slaves.

After some little time, we went out and inspected the fifty-five slaves, some of whom appeared quite happy at the prospect of a change; having already, as I had no doubt, experienced that they were in the hands of a fiend. My father then sent down a detachment, accompanied by a number of Darroola's men, to the canoes to bring up the requisite goods, and in the mean time the two chiefs returned to the drinking chamber, and seemed determined upon having a jollification. Darroola was, in his own way, very amusing, but I could hardly look at his savage countenance without wishing myself anywhere else than within his premises. The articles were soon brought up from the canoes; Darroola very generously ordered a cask of rum to be broached, and a good allowance to be served to all the men of both parties; and the whole afternoon was spent in jollity. My father, however, took the precaution, some time before sun-down, to go down to his canoes himself, and appoint a guard of fifteen men to watch all night: the others were to be accommodated at the palace.

We returned to the palace about dusk, and partook of a feast which did credit to Darroola's cooks. At the request of Darroola, a few of my father's men were brought into the room where the two chiefs sat, and allowed to sit down along with them, and partake of the good things; and in the course of the evening we were visited by a priest of the country, whom I instantly recollected having often seen at our own palace. After some time, this priest, who sat next my father, took a small idol out of his pocket, and holding it up, pretended to be whispering a prayer to it; but this was only to attract my father's attention without being suspected by Darroola: who, by the way, was busily plying some of our men with rum, and had his head and his attention turned in another direction. The priest then whispered, " King Zembola, listen to me, but look as if you heard not. You have been my friend; I am your friend: I cannot see you betrayed. Mark me now:—an attempt will be made to destroy you and your men to-morrow, when you are at the point of embarking: be on your guard. I can say no more. Now, do not let your countenance betray you. You are safe to-night; but to-morrow—remember to-morrow." I could instantly perceive my father's countenance change; but he quickly commanded his emotion, and looking steadily at the faithful old priest, merely pressed his hand, and said, " Good! my friend, I shall never forget you."

The entertainment continued, and at last all were more than ready for bed. Many, indeed, had already made theirs on the floor without ceremony, and King Darroola snored in his chair of state. My father and I retired to a room prepared for us; and after placing two sentinels at the door, and seeing that our arms were in order, we lay down to sleep, and did not awake until dawn of day. The two kings met in the morning with the greatest affability; and refreshments were soon prepared, which speedily carried off all the effects of last evening's revelry.

In the course of the forenoon, the fifty-five slaves were all taken down to the landing-place, coupled together with fetters; and all being settled at the palace, King Darroola and about a dozen of his men, unarmed, accompanied us, and we all proceeded to the shore: apparently in peace and kindness. The slaves were then placed in two of the canoes, and the troops belonging to my father were preparing to take their places; part having to go in the same canoes with the slaves, and the remainder with their chief and myself in our best canoe.

At this juncture, Darroola embraced me, and then my father, with seeming cordiality, wishing us a good voyage and a good market, and then retired up the bank a few paces. Presently, however, he turned round, and exclaiming,—" King Zembola, I forgot something," — he gave a signal, and in an instant fifty or sixty men sprang out with a yell from the brushwood about a hundred yards distant, and commenced firing with great celerity. My father, being so far on his guard, had told his men previously to have their muskets loaded, each with a ball and eight or ten buckshot; and he now very steadily told them to stand close and firm, and give the enemy a volley. At the first surprise, two of our party fell dead, but our men were superior in discipline to Darroola's, and better marksmen; as they proved by their first volley, which brought down from fifteen to twenty of the enemy. Our men, too, were furnished with bayonets, which Darroola's had not; and ere they could again load, my father, setting the example, called on his men to charge, which they did in gallant style, and in two minutes Darroola and his men were nearly out of sight. My father, however, was as cautious as he was brave, and not knowing how many more might be in ambush, he ordered us to embark without a moment's delay; and on our way down to the water, he ordered his men to despatch every one of the enemy who lay wounded. With the utmost speed we hauled out the whole of the canoes, and were soon at the farther side of the Congo, driving down the stream as fast as our paddles and the current could carry us.

My father sat in silence for a considerable space of time after we were afloat; but his countenance was altogether changed—it absolutely turned to a palish-grey hue, and his eyes rolled in their sockets as if they would burst from their orbits. At length his rage found utterance. He lifted up his hands, and swore by all the gods that were ever known in Africa, that he would not rest day or night until he had taken bloody revenge on Darroola and his tribe. " I have known," said he, " treachery practised by enemies on each other in war; but, in peace and friendship, never. Was there ever the equal to that accursed Darroola? By the Great Kolla! if I do not spill the blood of the whole tribe like water, may my whole race go to jumbo!" Then, by way of encouraging his men, he told them to broach a cask of rum, and gave each man a good cupful. He also gave the poor slaves a little to cheer their hearts, as they seemed evidently delighted at Darroola being put to flight. He then told the rowers to pull incessantly, promising them ample allowance of victuals and drink; and so well did all execute their task, that, by the evening of the next day, we were safe at our own landing-place.

After seeing the slaves secured, the first thing my father did was to go into the room where the hideous idol I formerly described was stationed, and give it a tremendous blow on the head with his cutlass. Although I put on a serious face, I could hardly help laughing at such conduct. He then called every male in the place to his presence, and after commenting a little on what had happened, he despatched messengers to every hut in his small domain, to summon instantly all who could wield a weapon. "That infernal scoundrel, Darroola," said he, "will expect me, as a matter of course; but I shall be upon him ere he imagines we are at home." He then allowed all to take rest for one night, but commanded that next morning there should be a general muster.

CHAPTER IV.

War Expedition—Zembola's Revenge—Burning a Negro Village—
Fight and Massacre.

WHEN the morning broke, my father's men began
to assemble from all quarters, and ere the sun was
two hours up not one of those expected were missing:
all seemed animated by the same spirit of retaliation
and revenge. A hundred and forty men were selected
for the enterprise, leaving about thirty in arms to take
charge of matters at home till the expedition returned. Five large canoes were put in order, and well
provided with victuals and liquor; ammunition, and
a quantity of combustible materials were provided,—
nothing, in short, that was requisite for our purpose
was omitted. By mid-day all were ready; and my
father, after giving orders to the person he left as his
representative, and taking farewell of my mother and
the rest of his wives and family, took me into the
room where the idol was placed, and kneeling down,
besought in a very earnest manner success on our
enterprise. For my own part, even at that time I
put very little faith in what the hideous image could

E

do,—more especially now, when his ugly head was nearly cloven in two. Alas! my poor father! may the only living and true God forgive thy ignorance, in the day when motives and not words shall be weighed.

We immediately afterwards embarked in the canoes, and set off at full speed, and both arguments and stimulants were used to make the rowers do their utmost. No untoward accident occurred to delay us for a moment, and in the afternoon of the third day we were within twenty miles of Darroola's village. The canoes were now brought close to the shore, and moored until the sun sank; immediately after which, having refreshed all hands, we again started, and orders were given that perfect silence should be maintained. About an hour before midnight we arrived within two miles of our destination; and here the canoes were brought close to the bank, and arrangements made for the attack.

As it was possible that Darroola might be even thus early on the watch, my father gave orders that twenty picked men, accompanied by myself, should endeavour to surprise the sentinels, who would probably be stationed near the landing-place; the remainder, including King Zembola, were to remain in arms beside the canoes, ready at a moment's warning for what might happen. I accordingly started with the twenty men, and as the night was exceedingly dark, and we were but partially acquainted with the ground, we had to choose our steps with caution. We marched right into the

country for about a quarter of a mile, then taking a
circuit, struck again down to the river side; and as we
approached the spot where we expected any sentinels
to be stationed, we crawled upon our hands and
knees, hardly daring to breathe. At last we could
perceive one man close to the river's bank, walking
backwards and forwards; and, still advancing, we
could make out three others sitting near him on the
ground, quietly smoking. Had King Darroola seen
them, their heads would no doubt have soon filled up
a few of his blank spaces on the pallisades. We now
all arose, but without the smallest noise, and rushing
forward, the four sentinels were secured and bound,
and threatened with instant death if a sound escaped
them. I despatched two swift-footed fellows to my
father, advising him to bring his men straight up by
the bank of the river; and such was their eagerness,
that in less than an hour our whole party had
joined us.

King Zembola now divided his whole force into
seven companies, of about twenty men each, and
every man of them was furnished with a few pitch-
pine splinters, prepared in a peculiar manner to render them more combustible, with directions that as
soon as they entered the village, and the signal was
given, each man was to set fire to the house nearest his station. My father then addressed a few
words to the whole of us, bidding us remember
that his honour, and the honour of our tribe, were at
stake, and that if we failed in taking signal vengeance on man, woman, and child, we were no

friends of his. " I shall sacrifice at least two hundred," said he, " and we shall have about as many left as prisoners : at all events, Darroola shall pay with his blood for his treachery. But spare the old priest you saw in conversation with me at Darroola's table. And now forward in quietness."

We marched in dead silence until we came to the village pallisades, and as fortune would have it, the first gate we came to yielded without force. The whole village was wrapt in deep repose and darkness, until the silence was broken by the barking of a dog or two. I felt considerably irritated at the treatment we had received from Darroola ; but, whether it was that my heart was formed of softer materials than my father's, or that a new light was beginning lately to break in upon my mind, certain it is I experienced an indescribable feeling—something allied to melancholy and sorrow—as I gazed around on the dwellings of the poor Kormantoos, who, though guiltless, and most of them totally ignorant of Darroola's treachery, would in a few minutes be aroused from their peaceful slumbers to all the horrors of fire, slaughter, and every species of murderous cruelty ; and although I calculated that a considerable number of prisoners would be our booty, I wished, from the bottom of my soul, that the injury could be otherwise atoned for. I had, however, hardly time to make these reflections before my father ordered me to station my company in front of Darroola's palace, saying that he would place his own company close to me, as we might expect most resistance there.

He then gave directions where the others should go, and told them that as soon as they saw a single torch blazing at his station, they were to light their torches with all expedition, and set fire to the nearest habitations.

In a few minutes afterwards, he struck a light himself, kindled a torch, and instantly our two companies held each his blazing torch aloft, and all the other companies followed like magic. The torches were no sooner applied to the dry thatch, or reeds, of which the huts were mostly formed, than the flames arose and spread like wildfire, and in a few minutes the whole village was in a blaze. And now arose the most awful shouting of men, mingled with the shrill screaming of women and children, that could be imagined; the terror-struck inhabitants endeavoured to rush out of their burning dwellings, but outside our men met them like infuriated tigers, and either cut them down with their cutlasses, or thrust them back into the flames with their bayonets. Some of the Kormantoo men made a gallant resistance, fighting with such weapons as they could snatch up in the confusion, but most of them were naked and unarmed, and of course had no chance. The palace windows were soon thrown open, and we could perceive Darroola himself, with a musket, at the head of a strong party of his men. They fired most determinedly, and even steadily, from the windows; but the flames made such rapid and fearful progress, that this warfare could not last long: a number of our men fell, and we could plainly see that our volleys

were thinning the number of our opponents within
the palace. At length the fire became so fierce, that
Darroola and his whole force of about thirty men,
made a sally from the front gate, and bravely met us
hand to hand. The struggle was now tremendous,
and many fell on both sides; at length Darroola
singled out my father, who by no means evaded him,
and for some time the two carried on a doubtful
combat. Darroola was armed with a huge battle-
axe, and my father with musket and bayonet parried
his blows with great dexterity, till at length my
father fairly thrust him through the body, and pinned
him against a wall of the palace : even in this horrible position the brave Darroola struck at his trium-
phant enemy; but his blows were now feeble, and
when my father withdrew his bayonet, his opponent
fell dead. Just as my father had finished this fierce
encounter, a ball from one of the enemy struck him
on the forehead, and ere I could reach him he had
fallen beside his enemy : he uttered only one groan,
and lay fixed in death. I was perfectly appalled,
and knew not what to do. The enemy still continued
to resist; but as the news of my father's death
spread through our ranks, most of the men came
hurrying to the spot, and I could perceive from their
numbers that we were completely victorious. I
instantly gave orders that mercy should be shown to
all who yielded.

Just at this moment, a young girl, with hardly any
clothing on her, but who, from the ornaments about
her head and neck, was evidently a person of rank,

came rushing up to me, followed by one of our men, who, with a cutlass uplifted, was in the act of striking her. I parried the blow and cried to him to desist; and, upon looking down, perceived the poor girl holding me by the feet and gazing imploringly in my face. By the light of the flames, I saw that she was beautiful, and as she turned up her eyes of heavenly sweetness, I could not help stooping down, and taking her in my arms, telling her that she was perfectly safe. I then told two of my men (for the men were now mine, alas!) to take her beside the other prisoners, and see that no harm came over her.

By this time day had broken, and of the beautiful village of Darroola hardly a vestige remained: a number of smoking heaps of ashes and rubbish, mingled with the remains of human beings, told where the cheerful and happy cottages had stood but yesterday; and the loud wailing and lamentation of the wretched prisoners would have melted the heart of any but a fiend. On mustering our men, I found that thirty-five were wanting, besides my father; whilst of Darroola's people at least two hundred must have fallen in all. Of prisoners, we had a hundred and thirty: many of these were children. I now gave orders to have my father's body laid decently aside and covered with a cloth, and then directed a search to take place for the bodies of our fallen countrymen: assisting in this work myself; and after considerable trouble we found twenty-six quite dead, and nine so severely wounded that they had little chance of seeing home. We speedily had a hole dug, in which we placed the bodies; and as I felt deeply touched by my father's death and the horrible carnage amongst our enemies, I prevailed upon my men, by the promise of some rum, to dig another large pit, and bury in it as many dead bodies of the poor Kormantoos as they could collect. We left none living, nor a roof remaining, in the village; and I believe that to this day the site remains a wilderness.

I was told that during the search for the dead, at the back of Darroola's palace (which I had not personally inspected), a low-built mud-walled hut was discovered, which had escaped the fire, from its being covered with flat stones instead of rushes as the other houses were, and that it had no windows, but only a very strong door. I instantly went to the spot with a few men, and, on forcing open the entrance, discovered a flight of steps which led down to a tolerably-sized vault or cellar. This proved to be Darroola's stronghold or treasury, and we found here a very considerable quantity of foreign goods, some casks of liquor, several very fine elephants' teeth, and, to our great satisfaction, a barrel containing between three and four thousand Spanish dollars, a hundred and twenty doubloons in a bag, and two small bags of gold-dust. Having brought out all these treasures, which were ours by right as conquerors, I had them placed in a heap on the outside; and collecting all my men, except the few who guarded the prisoners, I addressed them to this effect: I told them that now, as I had succeeded my father as their king, I intended to act towards all of them as a generous chief, and that I hoped they would ever be faithful and true to me; and that, as a proof of my feelings towards them, as soon as we arrived at home, I would divide the whole of the spoil (except one or two things which I would place in the royal treasury) equally and justly amongst all of them, and that the shares of the men who had fallen would be given to their widows or other relatives. This announcement was received with shouts of joy, and immediately the whole body of the men knelt down, and each holding both hands close to the crown of his head, swore aloud by the great God Kollah, that they would be true to the death to me and mine.

When I reflected, in after years, since the light of the blessed Gospel had shone into my benighted soul, upon this act of homage paid to me, I could not help sometimes weeping bitterly to think that I, at that time a poor ignorant boy, should accept of such reverence, which was due to God only. But, alas! at that time I was sitting in the darkness and shadow of death, and knew no better.

I then ordered a detachment of thirty men to go down and bring up our five canoes to the landing-place, where I would meet them with the prisoners, whom I immediately went to inspect. I found them generally in a most miserable plight; many of them, as they afterwards told me, looking for nothing less than death in some cruel and protracted manner: for such was often the custom with conquerors in this

part of Africa, so soon as they had leisure to enjoy
the horrid scene. I assured them, however, that,
much as we had been provoked by the treachery of
their chief, not one of them should suffer so long as
they behaved peaceably ; and, farther, I caused some
refreshment to be given them. The poor creatures,
one and all, testified their joy and gratitude at this
announcement, and capered and clapped their hands
with delight, as well as their bonds would permit
them.

I next inquired for the girl who had run to me for
protection the evening before, and found her seated
amidst a group of women, who had lent her some of
their clothing, and appeared to hold her in great
respect. At my approach, the poor girl rose, a blush
(for allow me, gentle reader, to assure you that
negroes really *can* blush as well as whites, although
not so perceptibly) spread over her cheeks, and she
seemed in great agitation. As our native languages
were nearly alike, I could readily make myself understood ; so, taking her by the hand, I inquired who
and what she was—for both her personal qualifica-
tions and the rich ornaments she wore convinced me
that she was no ordinary personage. She answered
at once that her name was Zillah; but here she
paused and held down her head, seemingly much
embarrassed. She then said that both her parents
were dead, and was proceeding, when I interrupted
her by saying,—" Oh ! never mind, Zillah, never
mind ; you can tell me all your history when I take
you to my mother." She seemed greatly relieved at

what she was pleased, in after days, to style my delicacy and feeling, and turned her beautiful eyes upon
me with a look of gratitude. The evening previous
to that I shall never forget : her looks had struck to
my heart with such force and influence as I had
never before experienced ; but now, in broad daylight, she appeared still more lovely and interesting,
and I gazed upon her for some time with a sensation
altogether new to me—pleasing beyond my power to
describe, and yet not without a degree of anxiety and
pain. In one word, love—all-powerful love—which
warms alike the hearts of kings and slaves, had
kindled in my breast. Yes, for the first time, and
after a scene of blood and cruelty, when my hands
were still red with gore (for I had, with my own
weapons, done some effectual service in the fray),
and while my heart was yet bleeding for the death of
my brave father, did the sweet and irresistible passion of love take possession of my soul.

Zillah appeared to be about a year or so younger
than myself. She was tall and exceedingly graceful,
her countenance—though its features were somewhat of the African cast—was beautiful, and her
figure might vie in elegance, colour excepted, with
the finest models of ancient sculpture. She wore
massive gold rings in her ears; a necklace of very
large pearls, mixed with gold and coral beads, adorned
her neck ; and solid bracelets of gold of African manufacture, and rings of the same metal, encircled her
wrists and ankles. I have little doubt but these jewels
would have brought 1000l. in Europe : it was the

sight of them that aroused the cupidity of the man
who was pursuing her; and had I not interfered at
the critical moment, the infuriated rascal would have
cut her down without mercy.

I now took Zillah, and telling her to choose out
two of her own sex to attend her, promised that I
would take her down the river in my own canoe; and
then ordered the whole party, my own men, prisoners
and all, to proceed to the landing-place.

And here I cannot help relating an affecting incident that occurred by the way. On the roadside lay
a young woman, cold in death, with a large wound in
her side, and at her breast was an infant endeavouring
to obtain its natural aliment from its dead mother's
bosom. I made one of the women take the child
along with her. No doubt, in last night's affray, the
poor mother had been mortally wounded while
endeavouring to escape, and death had overtaken
her here.

By the time we reached Darroola's landing-place,
our men had safely brought up the five canoes; and
as these would not have conveniently carried our now
increased company, we took three canoes which had
belonged to our late enemy, and after some little
trouble in arranging the prisoners, we proceeded
down the river: as a matter of course I brought
my father's body along with us. In three days we
reached our village; and some of our people (amongst
whom were two of father's wives and four of my sisters), who were waiting at the landing-place, perceived, as we approached, that something was wrong;

although they guessed, by the additional canoes, that
we had been successful.

We no sooner made known King Zembola's death,
than all was confusion and outcry, and in a few
minutes the whole village was in motion. I went
speedily up to the palace, taking Zillah by the hand,
and met my mother, whom I requested to go in with
me. In a few words, I acquainted her and the other
wives of my father with what had occurred. There
was now nothing but screaming, tearing of hair,
and other violent manifestations of grief. My mother,
however, at my earnest request, commanded her
feelings better than some of the other royal dames,
who had possibly less affection for my father. I
entreated my mother to take care of Zillah, and to
treat her as a daughter; and my mother, notwithstanding her grief, embraced the poor girl affection-
ately, and led her to an inner apartment. I immediately returned to the landing-place, to superintend
the removal of my father's body, and saw every one
ashore. I then appointed suitable guards to the
prisoners, and ordered arrangements for their safe
custody; for such was the irritation of our people,
both men and women, who had been left at home,
on learning the death of my father and so many of
his brave men, and at sight of the wounded (though
these were now actually amending) that they were with
difficulty prevented from falling upon some of the
poor prisoners, and taking summary vengeance. I
informed them, however, that enough revenge had

been already taken, and warned them, as they valued
the favour of their king, which I now was, to do the
prisoners no harm. I then, having got all our plun-
der ashore, made a fair and just distribution, as I
had promised ; and this, together with a moderate
supply of rum to all, had a great effect in promoting
peace and resignation. I may here remark, that the
value of dollars and of gold coin was perfectly understood in this part of the country ; and those who were
possessed of money had frequent opportunities of
exchanging it for goods with passing traders.

Having made other arrangements to the best of
my ability, I then gave orders that the body of the
late king should be consigned to its parent earth :
indeed, in such a climate, it had been already too long
above ground. I permitted all who chose to take a
last look of my father's corpse ; and a suitable grave
having been dug, we laid it in the ground with many
unmeaning ceremonies, and buried with it some of
the brave warrior's weapons. According to a custom
often put in practice here, one or two of my father's
wives insisted on being made a sacrifice, and interred
along with him ; but, partly by threats, and more by
promises to them and their children, I induced them
to forego this horrible piece of superstition. I could
not, however, prevent some of the wives and other
female domestics from making great gashes on their
bodies with knives and other instruments.

In the evening, I paid my respects to Zillah, and
was pleased to find that she had already made some

progress in my mother's affections. I left them together, after a few minutes, as all were much in want of refreshing sleep.

The next day, I requested my mother to go with me to the stronghold or cavern already mentioned; for I had found a large key in my father's pocket, and recollected his having told me that he had some valuables in his treasury which he could show me at any time. I must confess that I now felt a strong curiosity to see what was in the cave, and, as I shall presently explain, for a laudable purpose. My mother and I went accordingly, and having opened a large closet or apartment which was sunk in the wall of the cavern, we found a chest containing some silver plate, about five thousand Spanish dollars, about four hundred large gold pieces in a bag, and three bags of gold dust, besides some other valuable articles. I found, also, that the stronghold was well stored with foreign goods of every description requisite for our use, and more casks of rum and brandy than we might perhaps turn to good account.

On our return, I, by my mother's advice (which showed she was far from being a jealous or envious woman) and with all good will, called into the state-chamber my late father's four wives and my nine half-sisters, and informed them that they would find no difference in their treatment, occupations, or way of living, and that I would, in all respects, so conduct myself towards them, that they should find their loss the less severe. As an evidence of my good intentions towards them, and that they might, in small matters, feel themselves more independent, I informed them of what money was left in the treasury, and promised that I would give each of the four wives five hundred dollars, and a hundred to each of their daughters. I need hardly say that my generosity, as they called it, was greatly applauded. The rest of this day I spent in looking after matters out of doors, which need not be related.

In the evening, I paid a visit to Zillah; and since she had now been accommodated with more suitable apparel, the elegance of her appearance was by no means lessened. Need I describe how my heart palpitated and my hand trembled as I approached her, or descant upon her downcast and embarrassed looks as I gazed on her interesting countenance? Many of my readers, no doubt, have felt the powerful influences of love far beyond what my feeble pen can portray, and they will easily, therefore, appreciate my feelings when I say, that I was now deeply and irretrievably smitten by the charming Zillah. Captive though she was, and entirely in my power, I never for a moment indulged the idea of doing violence to her feelings or affections; but I burned with eager curiosity to know who she was. Taking her by the hand, I said,—" Now, sweet Zillah, you may perceive that I am interested in you more than words can express. Tell me, who and what were your parents?" Poor Zillah fell a trembling, and faltered out,—" What can I deny to the preserver of my life? Oh, my lord! if you could but imagine the gratitude with which my heart beats towards you, indeed you

would pity me. I dare not—I am afraid to utter
the truth ; for, alas! I shall incur your displeasure,
and you will drive me from your presence with horror."
—" Zillah !—dear Zillah ! allow me to call you—what
can this mean? It is all a mystery to me. It is
impossible, perfectly impossible, that you can have
reason to dread me. I look upon you as innocence
and purity itself. If there is a secret which you
dread to reveal, I swear to you that, whatever it may
be, it cannot—shall not—abate my love to you for
a moment."—" Well, then, my lord, since you speak
so generously, at the risk of all that is dear to me,
I shall no longer conceal from you who I am. My
lord,"—and here Zillah drew herself up with a dignity quite becoming—" I am the daughter of —
Darroola !" She burst into tears, and would have
fallen to the ground, had I not caught her in my
arms, and pressed her with fervour to my bosom.
" And so, Zillah," answered I, gazing on her sweet
countenance, " you were afraid, my own sweet Zillah!
—for mine you must be—to tell me of a circumstance that you could no more prevent than I can
help being the son of Zembola. Our fathers have
both fallen, even side by side, and though both of
them were wrong on many things, they fell like
brave and noble princes; and henceforth the loves
of Zillah and Zamba shall far, far outweigh the
hatred of Darroola and Zembola—shall it not be so,
dear Zillah ?" Zillah seemed quite overcome; and
looking up in my face with a beaming countenance,
said—" Noble-minded Zamba ! then am I happy.

F

You love me for myself; and it would be folly indeed to deny that your appearance, and your generous conduct from the first, raised a passion in my breast such as I never dreamt of before." I shall not enlarge upon this interview, for it is only to those immediately concerned that such scenes are interesting. Zillah, however, informed me, with a fresh flood of tears, that her mother was the unfortunate woman whose head Darroola had caused to be fixed on the pallisades of the palace on the morning of our first visit; but that her father's jealousy was utterly groundless. This circumstance only rendered her the more dear to me.

CHAPTER V.

Zamba settles at Home, and marries Zillah—Marriage Entertainments
—Searching for Gold Dust—Zamba encourages Agriculture—Learns
to read the Bible—His ideas of Christianity—He repels an Invasion.

I BEGAN now to think of the important station in
which I was placed; a youth of seventeen, with so
many dependants, also all looked up to me for
directions. The great number of prisoners on hand
gave me much concern. I saw plainly that I could not
keep them all about me; but, in the mean time, I set
such of them as were able to do a little work in the
fields. The stubborn and idle disposition of most
of them, however, proved to me that I should be
obliged to make a bargain with Captain Winton for
them on his next arrival. But when I came to consider whether or not I was to pursue business as my
father did, I found that my feelings and inclinations
were not in unison with his. I was not, I believe,
deficient in animal courage, nor in ambition, altogether; but the horrors of the burning of Darroola's
village caused in me an aversion to war in any
shape. If an enemy attacked me in my own dominions I would have fought to the last; but I
revolted from the systematic practice of going out

F 2

regularly with trained warriors, for the purpose of
picking a quarrel with some weaker neighbour, and
plundering him,—especially when I was convinced
that by peaceably cultivating the earth, fishing in
the waters, or hunting upon land, my people and I
could procure sufficient for all our ordinary wants.
Besides these, there was the chance of finding gold
in a tolerable quantity, if it were carefully sought
for. At all events, without going to war for the
purpose of procuring slaves, I had capital enough to
carry on trade on a large scale. But the idea of
visiting some civilized countries, and attaining a
knowledge of their customs and religion, was ever
present to my mind: even my new-born affection
for Zillah could not wholly eradicate these thoughts.
Notwithstanding, my love for her continued daily to
increase, and we enjoyed all the delightful sensations
which innocent intercourse, and the anticipation of
future happiness could bestow; for we resolved, that
out of respect to our deceased parents, we would put
off our union for at least three moons. Even yet, in
my old age, and in a land far from my native Africa,
I often recur to the delightful walks we enjoyed together on the banks of the Congo. But I must not
anticipate my history.

About two months after King Zembola's death,
Captain Winton arrived, and pretended to feel great
sorrow at the loss of his old friend. By dint of
persuasion, and some presents, I persuaded him to
stay with us for two weeks, and during this time I
got him to give me daily lessons in reading; and by

great attention and perseverance I made astonishing progress, as the captain averred. I could now read any common English book with tolerable facility; although many words, and even sentences, were as yet wholly unintelligible to me. I obtained from him, likewise, as much information regarding foreign countries as our time would permit. At length Captain Winton asked me plainly whether I would take a trip with him to America? saying, that he would then take me to London, where he was in the habit of doing business, and bring me back to my own country again. This idea pleased me mightily; but at present the thoughts of Zillah, and the necessity that pressed on me to settle affairs rightly in my own kingdom, prevented my going with him. He said, that by shipping a good lot of slaves, and taking what gold dust I had in store, they would bring me quite a fortune in America; that I could invest it in produce there—all which matters he would assist me in to the utmost; and by taking that produce to England, and purchasing manufactured goods in that country with the proceeds, I could finally land in Africa with property equal to any king in South Africa. I told him I should seriously think of all this: never for a moment doubting his sincerity. Captain Winton now made a bargain with me for the whole of my prisoners that were disposable: for there was a considerable number of infants and some others that I thought proper to retain. He bought between eighty and ninety, and in sending them away I never doubted but that I was doing them a service.

I now commenced preparations for my marriage with Zillah; and as it is not every day that a king's marriage takes place, even in wild Africa, where so many petty chiefs assume that lofty appellation, these preparations were upon a large scale. I first signified my intentions to my privy council—for I actually had a select number of my officers, and a few of the eldest and most experienced men in my dominions, whom I had formed into a body, with whom I consulted upon all important occasions— and then despatched messengers to invite several neighbouring monarchs to the wedding. In particular I did not forget King Gooloo Bambo; and being certain that he would come equipped in the manner formerly described, I charged my envoy to inform him in a quiet way that he would oblige and honour me greatly by adding breeches to his costume; and as a token of my friendship, I sent him a very elegant pair for the occasion. The envoy had some difficulty in making Gooloo understand the propriety of such a proceeding, and his Majesty made some objections to this innovation; when, however, it was signified to him that if he did not comply with my request in this small matter, there would be very little strong waters coming his way in the entertainment, he at once gave in, saying, "Oh, Golly! Golly!— Can't want plenty rum at King Zamba's marriage: —must after all put on him breeches like de buckrah man."

After I had fixed the important day, one morning, as I held a kind of levee, my two friends Pouldamah

and Bollah, who saved my life by shooting the lion
who had his paw on me, entered the audience-
chamber and prostrated themselves before me; then,
rising up, in a hesitating manner, said they had a
petition to prefer to me, and begged in the most
humble manner that, provided I thought proper to
refuse their suit, I would at all events not punish
them severely. When I bethink myself now, how
that I, at that time little more than a boy, could
accept, and accept with pleasure and pride, such
homage—indeed, it might be called worship—from
my fellow-men, I cannot but smile at the weakness
of man on the one hand, and his arrogance on the
other. Truly I deserved the reprobation of Providence for my presumption. The two young men
then gave me to understand that they had gained the
affections of my two half-sisters, Zedra and Koo-
lamah, at whose instance, and with the consent of my
own mother, they now petitioned to have their marriages celebrated along with my own. As I have
always considered that a favour granted is only half
a favour when granted reluctantly, and as my sym-
pathies at this critical period were peculiarly tender
in love matters, I at once acceded to their request;
telling them that no doubt they would henceforth be
as ready as ever to peril their lives for me. It is
almost needless to add, that I received the warmest
assurances of their affection and gratitude.

My wedding-day at length arrived, and, to use the
language of white men, I was " made happy;" and
so were five other individuals, if I might judge from

appearances. The marriages were celebrated by the
old priest who had proved so friendly to my father
in the matter of Darroola's treachery, and who was
accompanied by a brother in the same "sacred"
office. The whole ceremony consisted of a few sense-
less mummeries, performed before a hideous idol,
and various invocations to the devil not to harm
the newly married people in any way—to remain
neutral, as it were. They neither asked nor expected
interposition on his part. These were accompanied
by certain rites, of such a nature that I cannot with
propriety attempt a description of them. There were
a great number of strangers present, and feastings and
rejoicings of one kind or another were kept up for ten
days : nor did night bring a cessation to the uproar;
for so I must term great part of the festival. An
African holiday is chiefly distinguished by uncouth
and incessant noise—firing of muskets, beating of
drums, blowing of horns, rattling of cymbals and tam-
bourines, and by the human voice in all the various
modulations of shouting, screaming, and yelling.

During the festival, various public entertainments
were given by lamp-light; and the large cave before
described served very well as the arena of the per-
formances. One night, the entertainment consisted
in a number of men disguised to represent various
wild and tame animals, chiefly quadrupeds; though a
good many figured as the fowls of heaven. The performers were dressed in the skins of the several
creatures intended to be represented, and some of
them played their parts with great credit to them-

selves and to the infinite satisfaction of the audience. The chief lion performed his part most nobly, and actually might almost have passed in twilight for a real monarch of the woods: he lashed with his tail, shook his mane, stamped with tremendous dignity, and roared tremendously. Several large baboons frisked and sported with great spirit, and a huge crocodile snapped his jaws, and beat his tail on the ground like a fury: a peacock and two large turkey-cocks also played their parts well. The whole at last joined in a kind of dance, or rather a stately promenade, bowing, and chattering, and roaring to each other with great complacency. In the midst of this singular masquerade, in came King Gooloo Bambo, in his full accoutrements, riding upon the back of a real living tame ostrich of enormous size, which he had trained for such occasions. His majesty was at least " half-seas-over," as the sailors say, and held a cup in one hand, and a large bottle in the other, with which he first helped himself, and drank to the health of all concerned, and then very generously helped each and all of the performers, some of whom, with difficulty, managed to raise the cup to their lips. I need not say that his majesty's performance was greatly applauded by all present. Another night a drama was represented in a rude way. At last the festivities came to an end, and all retired to their respective homes well satisfied: to my great relief; for the last ten days had made a fearful inroad upon my provision stores, and especially upon the spirit casks, which were brought to a very low ebb.

On the last night of the festival I made a speech to my brother chiefs, thanking them for their attendance, and signifying my desire henceforth to live on terms of the strictest amity with all of them; and that I intended to avoid all occasion of going to war, unless in extremity, or in self-defence. But as there were some of them who, I was convinced, held me rather low in their estimation on account of my pacific principles, I declared that should any king or tribe attack me unprovokedly, they might perhaps find me not unprepared for war to the utmost.

As soon as we had again all become a little tranquillized after the excitement of our marriage festival, I began to put my kingdom in order. I determined to keep up the standing army to its former amount, but at the same time I obliged my warriors to spend at least one-half their time in the cultivation of small plots of land which I gave them; or in hunting, fishing, or searching for gold dust. I found, however, that although I allowed them many indulgences, they had still a great longing after war expeditions; and I could learn, in a quiet way, that they often drew comparisons by no means to my advantage, between my father's warlike propensities and what they called my unmanly disposition. I also made my two brothers-in-law a present of so much land as would engage their attention, and keep them comfortable, and also gave them sundry stores and utensils to commence with; and, farther, appointed them to stations of trust near my royal person. I afterwards made several trading excursions up the river, and drove many bargains with white traders, who now frequently visited me.

I had, in company with my brothers-in-law, made a valuable discovery of gold dust. In the ravine before mentioned, where I had the adventure with a baboon, I remarked that there were a great many excavations or pits in the bed of the stream. It may not perhaps be known to all my readers, that what is called gold dust by the trading world, is not a powder like flour, or the dust of the earth, or ground coffee, but is found in grains from the size of a pin's head to that of a common pea, or even larger. The way in which we collected it was by taking a few handfuls of sand and gravel from the bed of the stream—especially where we could evidently perceive the glittering particles—and placing the whole on a calibash, or small wooden vessel, which was held under a slender stream of water, we kept incessantly shaking it and turning it over with our hands. The lighter particles, of course, were swept by degrees over the edge of the vessel, and after a little time our patience was generally rewarded by a few pieces of the precious metal which sank to the bottom; many small particles, however, escaped in such a rude and simple operation. I had become acquainted with the mysterious power of the loadstone, through the instructions of Captain Winton (who also made me a present of several magnets), and it occurred to me that were some substance discovered which would attract particles of gold in the same way that small pieces of iron were attracted by the loadstone, it would be a great

advantage indeed to gold-dust hunters. I also bethought me, that by searching at the bottom of the
deepest hollows in the bed of the stream, I should
have a better chance of finding gold dust than
hitherto. We therefore set to work, and after re-
moving two or three feet in depth of round gravel
and rubbish, we operated upon the soil we found
undermost, and were astonished at the quantity of
gold dust which in this way had been accumulating
in those natural vessels for ages. I now had regular
gangs of workers sent to this stream, and to stimulate
them the more, I gave a certain portion to each slave
of all that they found, or else some equivalent from
my stores. In this way, during the first year after
my marriage, I had collected as much as a hundredweight of the precious metal, the greatest part of
which I exchanged with traders for European goods,
so that my stores were amply replenished.

About a year after our marriage, Zillah brought me
a son and heir to the throne. Soon afterwards
Captain Winton arrived, bringing with him many
rarities as presents; amongst others, some very fine
articles of apparel for me. I bargained with him for
a number of slaves, some gold dust, and a few elephants' teeth; but, although I had been thinking
much on the subject, I could not yet bring my mind
to think of going with him to sea; principally on
account of my love to Zillah, which suffered no
diminution. I talked over the matter with him,
however, again and again, and it still ran in my
mind that sooner or later go I must, at all hazards.

At this visit, which lasted a fortnight, I gave Winton some very valuable presents, and insisted on his spending most of the day in giving me further lessons in reading; so that I could now read English with more ease and accuracy than would be readily believed. I also managed to get considerable information from him regarding the Christian religion, although he seemed by no means greatly interested in the matter. The captain perceiving how well he had brought me on by his former lessons and my own indefatigable perseverance—for my heart was in the matter—prepared to leave me the elements and the sum of all truth, namely, the Bible; and he did leave me a very handsome one. I got him to explain a few of the leading points of Scripture, but I could see plainly that some other teacher than Captain Winton was awanting. He, however, by word of mouth, gave me a cursory view of the first two or three chapters of Genesis, and then recommended me to begin and go through the New Testament.

After Winton went away I made it a rule to read a part of the Holy Scriptures every day, and although the light which I had to guide me in this was but as the glimmering of a glow-worm, and I knew not how to ask assistance from on high in the right way—that is, through Jesus, who alone is the way, the truth, and the life; yet I do hope and believe that my heavenly Father, perceiving the sincerity of my heart, and the peculiarity of my situation, occasionally shed a bright ray of light from on high to guide me in my darkened and miserable condition.

There were, however, many words and expressions of which I could by no means make out the literal English meaning, much less could I understand the spiritual signification. I had no one to whom I could refer in my difficulty, and as yet I wanted one who could teach me to pray.

It may be interesting to the reader to know what were my ideas at this time regarding Christianity, as being derived by an unassisted heathen from the sacred pages. I felt that the life and character of Jesus Christ were totally different from those of all other men whom I could conceive had ever lived before: that he was altogether pure and spotless; that in no case did he ever seek his own aggrandizement in a worldly sense—rejecting the offers of men to make him a king; that he went about continually doing good, and performing before thousands such miracles as were quite unheard of previously in the world. It occurred to me also that he who could feed thousands with a few loaves and small fishes, who could calm the raging sea, and raise the dead from the grave, could also, if he willed, have called up an army of men from the dust of the ground; but in place of this, he forbade his followers to fight in his defence, and delivered himself up calmly to the rage of his enemies: and all this that he might save from some awful future calamity the whole race of sinful and wicked mankind. To die for his worst enemies, and even to pray for those who were the immediate instruments of his death, seemed to me altogether so different from the way of the world, as

far as I had seen or heard, that I conceived such a
sublime and uncommon idea could arise only in the
mind of some being altogether superior to the human
race.

The more I perused the Bible, the more could I
discern that it must have been a book sent from
heaven to instruct blinded and wicked men, and to
lead them to look beyond the mere matters of this
world to something more glorious in another state of
existence; for even in heathen Africa we had some
faint glimmerings of a future state, where good men
would be rewarded, and those who had been very
wicked in this world would be punished.   I could
also begin to perceive that my heart was exceedingly
inclined to follow after that which was evil, and that
I had hitherto acted upon a very different principle
from that golden rule which the Saviour laid down;
namely, to do unto all men as they would that all
men should do unto them.

There were many expressions of our Saviour's which
at this time extremely puzzled me, though I humbly
hope that many, many years since they have appeared to me as clear as the sun at noonday.   But in
my early years, and without an interpreter, I took
the meaning literally as it was expressed.   I could
not understand that He who was meekness and benevolence itself, and who brought " peace on earth and
goodwill to men," should in another place say, that
he " came not to send peace, but to bring a sword
upon earth, and to set the father against the son and
the son against the father;" nor why, elsewhere, he

should recommend us to cut off our hand, or pluck
out our eye if it offended us. Neither could I altogether understand how we were to forsake all and
follow him. But at this time I was blind, and could
by no means comprehend the spiritual interpretation
of scripture. It is no doubt owing to hardness of
heart that thousands of civilized men, who have
every opportunity of deriving life and light from the
pages of the Bible, merely glance at it occasionally
when the pressure of worldly pursuits slackens for
a few minutes, and without entering into the matter
heart and soul, are content to pick out an expression
here and there; never troubling themselves to com-
pare one part with another and consider the whole
as a divine revelation, but in their carelessness and
apathy becoming more confused in their ideas of salvation, they again recur to the world, seeking for comfort and consolation in worldly pleasures and pursuits,
and losing their way in the vague and dense mists of
infidelity.

At this period I attempted to communicate a few of
my newly acquired ideas to my mother and Zillah,
who listened to me very patiently; but I could perceive that it was only their affection for me that secured
their attention: they shook their heads, and said,
" White man's religion too deep." Any light, alas!
which I could throw on the matter was feeble indeed: it was the blind leading the blind. From
this time, however, I renounced my household idols,
and never once entered the room where they were
stationed. At the same time, until I saw more clearly

how I could bring my friends to perceive the beauty and glory of the doctrine of Jesus, I considered there would be little good attained in depriving them of that small consolation which they appeared to derive from the worship of those false gods.

About two months after his birth, our child, my heir apparent, died, to the great grief of Zillah and myself. I, however, continued improving the condition of my people, and adding to my own stores daily from the increased trade I was carrying on; but I soon found that an earthly crown is not always worn with both honour and ease. I had sent my brother-in-law, Pouldamah, with a canoe and ten men to carry an assortment of goods to a chief named Cumanay, about a hundred miles up the river, with instructions to trade. Pouldamah accomplished this part of his mission satisfactorily, and both he and his men were hospitably entertained and feasted. It happened, however, that one evening some of his men and those of the king my neighbour had become merry with drink, and were boasting of the qualities of their respective chiefs. In the course of their talk, some of my neighbour's men called me " a woman," and said I was afraid to go to war; adding that I should not reign long over any except women like myself. My men were nearly coming to blows at last, when one of the opposite party, who was furious with drink, hinted pretty broadly that I should have a visit not altogether to my liking next new moon. My men looked upon this merely as a drunken boast, but related all to me on their return, and I

G

considered it prudent, therefore, to be on my guard.
I had my men daily exercised; all our arms were
kept in order, in case of any attack; and the whole
of my best warriors were warned to be ready at a
minute's notice.   At the time expected, I set a watch
at night by the river-side, and kept a look-out through
the day; and on the first evening of the new moon,
the whole of my forces were assembled at sun-down,
close to the river-side, and kept watch during the
whole night.   About an hour before daybreak, some
of my people could hear the noise of paddles on the
water, and just at daybreak we could perceive ten or
twelve canoes full of men approaching our landing-
place, most of whom I could observe were armed.
There was no mistaking their intention.   I had made
most of my men conceal themselves amongst the
bushes, and by allowing my enemy to approach within
forty or fifty yards of the shore, I could suddenly have
opened a most deadly and destructive fire upon them;
but the new light which had dawned upon my heart,
influencing my naturally peaceable disposition, inclined me to avoid the wanton effusion of blood; as
soon, therefore, as the hostile fleet came within about
three hundred yards, I ordered the whole of my men
who had muskets to give at once a complete volley,
which I knew at such a distance would frighten, but
not prove very fatal to my foes.   The first volley
staggered them, and by the time we had repeated the
salute three or four times, our enemy had fairly
turned tail; and we could perceive, from certain
unequivocal yells, that some of them were wounded.

They were out of sight in an hour; and I had the further gratification of finding that my merciful procedure was very advantageous to me, even in the opinions of my brother chiefs. Some time afterwards, meeting King Cumanay at a neighbouring station, where I was trading, I reproached him with his unfair and unworthy attack upon one with whom he had no cause of complaint; when, to my astonishment, he firmly denied having any part in the transaction, and swore by all his idols that it must have been some other tribe who had so basely endeavoured to take advantage of me. Seeing how matters stood, I did not insist upon the accusation, but signified that I should be ready at all times for any treacherous enemy, and that the next time my assailants would not be let off so cheaply. During the time I remained in Africa after this affair, I had no further annoyance from my neighbours; so far verifying the adage of more civilized men, that to be prepared for war in time of peace is the truest wisdom.

CHAPTER VI.

Zamba embarks for America—Interior of a Slave-Ship—Voyage—Treacherous designs of Captain Winton—Arrival at Charleston—Sale of
Slaves—Zamba is plundered and sold as a Slave—Reflections on his
condition.

CAPTAIN WINTON arrived soon after this matter had
occurred, and as usual we traded to a large extent.
I at last told him that my curiosity was so excited on
various subjects, that I should most likely be ready
to accompany him in his next voyage. Some time
after this, Zillah brought me another son; but, like
the first, he only survived a few months; and this
circumstance, although it by no means lessened my
affection for my wife, increased my desire to go
abroad. Nothing remarkable occurred for a considerable time; and towards the end of the season,
when Captain Winton again made his appearance, I
decided to make my long-projected voyage. As I
have always conceived that evil, whether to ourselves
or others, comes soon enough without anticipating it,
I had never hinted either to Zillah or my mother
anything regarding my intention of leaving Africa;

and now that I told them of my determination, they
were of course in great grief, and used every endear-
ing art to detain me.   But I was firm to my purpose;
and at length some of my arguments, and the promise
of my return, had the effect of pacifying them a little.
I arranged all my government affairs, and appointed
my two brothers-in-law to act as regents in my
absence, either jointly or separately.

Captain Winton was very anxious that I should
put on board all the gold dust and other African
produce that I possessed, and as many slaves as I
could muster.   I was not, however, blind to the
imprudence of such a course: the ship might be lost,
or I might be cut off by sickness or accident; and in
either case I should be doing great injustice to my
family to incur the loss of so much treasure.   I
therefore shipped only a part of my property ; namely,
thirty-two prime slaves, about thirty pounds of gold
dust, and somewhat over two hundred doubloons in
gold coin.   The captain had brought me a farther
supply of clothing, both fine and coarse, which, with
some African rarities and my gold, were stowed in
two fine trunks that Winton made me a present of.
He seemed, indeed, as if he could not do enough for
my accommodation; and had I only possessed a
little more shrewdness, and been less inexperienced
in the ways of this deceitful world, I should have
perceived that he had some underhand intentions in
regard to me.

After many tears and lamentations on both sides,
and an assurance on my part that after visiting

America and England, I should return with Captain
Winton, bringing home as much property as would
make me the richest king on the banks of the Congo,
I bade adieu to Zillah and Africa.   Little did I then
think that I should no more see dear Africa for ever!
My mother told me, as she bade me farewell, that,
from certain dreams she had, she was convinced she
should behold my face no more; and poor Zillah was
inconsolable.   At this distant date, I now think of
all this with a melancholy kind of satisfaction, yet
with a natural regret; but when I reflect upon the
way in which a merciful Providence has acted towards me, I feel my heart swell with gratitude and
love.   Out of seeming evil, how much good hath
fallen to my lot is not to be reckoned.   The Almighty
in His wisdom thought fit to wrest from me a few
handfuls of yellow glittering dust; but He hath since
repaid me with that inestimable treasure, which is
from heaven, which no one can rob me of, and which
will never perish, nor rust, nor fade away.

Captain Winton accommodated me with a handsome state-room, and we left the Congo on the first
day of October 1800.   I found that, including my
own thirty-two, there were in all four hundred and
twenty-two slaves on board: but as the vessel was of
500 tons burthen, they were not so crowded for space
as I have since learned has often been the case with
emigrants from Europe to America; their accommodation, however, was very miserable.   The ship's
lower deck was divided fore and aft into compart-
ments of about six feet square, by planks raised

about six inches; and into each of these divisions four
slaves were put; to lie down, or sit, or take it as they
chose. The planks were intended to keep them
from rolling when the sea was rough. Of course,
they had nothing but the hard deck to lie upon.
In regard to clothing they were very scantily supplied: in general, both male and female had a yard
and a half, or two yards of Osnaburghs wrapped round
their loins; and some of them had a piece of cloth,
or a handkerchief, bound round their heads. The
males were all linked two and two by a small chain
round the ankle. As for provisions, they were much
better off than in the generality of slave-ships; and
this, strange as it may appear, they owed to the
avarice rather than the humanity of the captain.
The motives of the latter, however, were of little
moment to the poor slaves, provided the end was for
their advantage. The slaves were supplied for breakfast with a fair ration of ground Indian corn boiled,
with a spoonful of molasses to each; they generally
had boiled rice for dinner; and supper was the same
as breakfast. Sometimes for dinner they received
each about half a pound of ship biscuit, with a little
morsel of beef or pork; too much of this latter would,
no doubt, have created thirst. Although this captain (as will be shown in the sequel of my narrative)
acted in a most dishonourable and treacherous manner towards me, and was totally devoid of all Christian principle, yet, to serve his own ends in the
matter of the slaves, he acted the part of a humane
and considerate man. He told me, in the course of

our voyage, that, in the early part of his experience
in the slave-trade, he had seen as many slaves as he
had with him at present shipped on board a vessel of
200 tons, where they were literally packed on the top
of each other; and, consequently, from ill air, con-
finement, and scanty or unwholesome provision, dis-
ease was generated to such an extent that in several
cases he had known only one-half survive to the end
of the voyage; and these, as he termed it, in a very
unmarketable condition. He found, therefore, that,
by allowing them what he called sufficient room and
good provisions, with kind treatment, his speculations
turned out much better in regard to the amount of
dollars received ; and that was all he cared for.

For the first few days, the most of us—I mean the
blacks—were laid down with sea-sickness : but, the
weather being fine, that was soon got over. The
captain caused the hatches to be kept open night and
day (except only upon two occasions) during the
whole voyage; and after daylight set in he allowed
about one-fourth of his cargo to come on deck for
two hours by rotation. He had always four of his
men, with loaded muskets and fixed bayonets, day
and night on deck ; but during this trip there never
was the slightest attempt at rioting and mutiny.
The only misfortune that befell us was this:—After
being about fifteen days out at sea, one evening,
about sunset—the ship with all sail set, going down
the trades at the rate of five knots an hour—in the
clap of a hand, or at least more suddenly than a
stranger to these latitudes could imagine, a heavy

squall struck the ship, carrying away great part of the loftier spars and sails, and laying her very nearly on her beam ends. In a few minutes a tremendous sea rose, and although the squall blew over in about a quarter of an hour, and the ship regained her position, the poor slaves below, altogether unprepared for such an occurrence, were mostly thrown on the lee-side, where they lay heaped on the top of each other; their fetters rendered many of them help-less, and before they could be arranged in their proper places, and relieved from their pressure on each other, it was found that fifteen of them were smothered or crushed to death, besides a great num-ber who were cruelly bruised. The captain seemed considerably vexed; but the only (or at least the chief) grievance to him was the sudden loss of some five or six thousand dollars.

Soon after I had recovered from sea-sickness, and was able to go about, one day at dinner-time I asked Captain Winton (who, though tolerably attentive to me, no longer showed that assiduous deference which he showed towards me in Africa) if he would give me a few lessons in reading the Bible, when he was not engaged in his duties. He looked with a peculiar expression to his chief mate, and smiled in a very significant manner, saying,—" You see, Mr. Prince (the mate's name), what a good Christian I have made of this King Zamba; you see how eager he is about the Bible. I question much if any of your missionary folks, who have been labouring for years to convert the heathen, have performed such a miracle as I have. And don't you think, Prince, that I deserve payment for my labour as well as ever a black coat amongst them?" Then addressing me, he said,—" Really, King Zamba, I must charge you for all the lessons I have given you for these some years past, and I cannot charge you less than a doubloon per hour. I could positively have picked up many a good boat-load of niggers during the time I spent in hammering lessons into your head ; and besides this, it is not every day that the poor master of a slave-ship falls in with a king for a pupil. We shall talk of this again, however, and settle our accounts at the end of the voyage." He laughed heartily as he said this, which I at first thought he meant only for a joke; but as he cast his eyes in a peculiar way from me to the mate, and again from the mate towards me, I could not help feeling somewhat uneasy. I felt, in fact, that I was not exactly safe. The captain, however, and sometimes Mr. Prince, the mate, listened to me whilst I read for an hour or so ; and they also gave me a few lessons in geography, and explained many very wonderful things to me.

About eight days after the circumstance related above, I had retired early to my berth, which was next the cabin. The upper part of the state-room door was of glass, and slid aside for ventilation, and a red curtain hung over it. As I lay awake about ten o'clock, ruminating upon my condition, the captain and Mr. Prince came down to consult their books and charts, and after a while the captain ordered the steward to bring in some liquor. They

sat for a considerable time conversing about the
affairs of the ship and the voyage; but at last I
could hear the captain say, in a low voice, " Look
in quietly, Prince, and see if his majesty is asleep,
but don't disturb him." On hearing the mate
approach my berth, I lay quite still, and breathed
hard, as if I were in deep slumber. Prince raised
the curtain, and called me two or three times in a
low tone, and then touched me on the shoulder, but
I still lay seemingly unconscious. He then retired,
and said, laughingly, to the captain, " Oh, poor
Zamba is as sound as a top; no doubt he is dreaming of hunting lions, or gathering gold dust in
Africa."—" Well, well," said Winton, " let him enjoy himself while he may; I rather fear, however,
that before long I shall awaken him to certain realities
which he little dreams of. Do you know, Prince,
that I have been thinking to make this voyage turn
out to be the best ever I made. " I have the hank in
my hand," as they say in Connecticut, and more fool
will I be to let slip the advantage. Betwixt niggers,
gold dust, and doubloons, this black fellow has more
than twenty thousand dollars; and what the deuce
is the use of all that to him? I really think, between man and man, that I have given him twenty
thousand dollars' worth of good English and sound
religion. As the parsons say, I have given him the
' Pearl of great price'—I have given him what gold
cannot purchase; and surely, Prince, ' the labourer
is worthy of his hire.' I shall at all events secure
the *dust* before many days go by." Although using

the words of sacred scripture, the avaricious rascal
said all this in a half-laughing tone. " But," said
Prince, " will not Zamba expose you, and tell the
whole story when he gets to Charleston ?"—" Expose, and be d——d !" answered Winton. " Are
you such a flat, Prince, as not to know that the
oath of a black or coloured man, ay, or of ten thousand of them, against a white man in Carolina is not
worth the seventh part of a d—n? No; although
a white man should cut the throats of a dozen niggers, and a thousand black fellows witnessed it, their
evidence would be no more regarded than the yelp
of a dog. Besides, Prince, just consider that this
black king, as they call him, has all his life had no
scruples in making merchandise of his own flesh and
blood. He thinks little just now, however, that the
fate of the thirty-two negroes he shipped on board
will be his own before a month's over. I have helped
at least to make him a sort of Christian, and now I
shall finish, Prince, by giving him a *great moral
lesson*—what think you ?" They had some farther
conversation after this which I could not exactly
make out; I had heard enough, however, as the
humane reader may well imagine, to awaken me,
indeed, to a sense of the horrible predicament into
which I had brought myself, and I could with difficulty prevent my sobs from being heard.

At the breakfast-table next morning I endeavoured
to command my feelings, so as that my countenance
might appear as usual; but Captain Winton remarked
that something was the matter with me. I told him I

was suffering much from headache. " Oh, Zamba,"
said he, " I know well enough what is the matter
with you; you have been dreaming about Africa and
your young wife : but keep up your heart, boy, you
will find plenty of pretty wives in Charleston. And,
by-the-by, Zamba, you will then see what you have
never seen before,—that is, women called mulattoes,
half white and half black—very pretty girls, I can
assure you ; they will be ready to snap at a king of
such property as you." But I was in little humour
for language of this sort. After breakfast I said that
I wanted to bathe my head with vinegar, and lie
down for a while ; and Winton making no objection,
I retired shortly afterwards to my berth. In the
course of the forenoon I contrived to conceal about
thirty of my doubloons, by sewing them in betwixt
the lining of various articles of my clothing ; I also
put a little gold dust away in the same manner, but
only amongst my coarse clothes, as I looked for
nothing less at this cruel captain's hands than to
have my fine clothing taken from me. I also stowed
away about two pounds weight of gold dust in each
of a pair of stockings, which I thrust carelessly
into a pair of shoes. Should I save these articles
from the clutches of my white " friend" Winton, I
calculated that it would be so much, at all events, to
help me in a strange land.

On the third day after this I was conning over a
chapter in the New Testament, when I came to that
place where it says, " What shall it profit a man to
gain the whole world, and lose his own soul ?" I

was forcibly struck with the mysterious ways of Providence. " If God," thought I, " has seen fit to permit this white man to rob me, and betray me for the sake of my money, am I not now in the way of having my precious soul everlastingly saved? So that, although it be partly through the means of a wicked and unprincipled man, who has made use of the precious words of scripture, and assumed the character of a follower of Christ, to entrap and betray me, I can yet see the hand of God in it all : out of seeming evil he can bring good; and thus all things redound to his glory. And as regards my slaves, let me ask my own heart, whether or not I have been doing as I would be done by? I now feel that I have fallen into the pit that I had digged for others; and I plainly see that—as if to prove the truth of the words of scripture, and to bring conviction home to my heart—Providence is allowing Captain Winton to measure out to me in the same way as I have been measuring out to others." And for the first time, I believe, I uttered an audible prayer, as I murmured to myself, " Lord have mercy upon me, and pardon me, and save me from the evils that I deserve. I cast myself before Thee, and can only say, God be merciful to me a sinner!"

These meditations were interrupted by the captain coming down, seemingly in a hurry; " Zamba, Zamba! " says he, " there is a vessel just now in sight, and I have my suspicions that she is a pirate— that is, a sea robber. Now the first thing they do is to search the cabin for money, and your trunks will be opened; you had, therefore, better give me your bag of gold dust and your gold pieces, all but a few, which you can reserve to offer to the pirates when they come. Now make haste, for it will take me a few minutes to put them in a safe place." What could I do but quietly surrender the gold? With sparkling eyes, and a grin of cunning delight, he took my treasure into his own state-room, and I never again cast my eyes upon it. In a few minutes the vessel neared us, and proved to be a Spanish slaver from Havannah, bound for the coast of Africa. We continued our course to westward and northward; and low-spirited as I was, I could not but be amused and interested by the wonders which are to be seen by those " who go down to the sea in ships."

At meal-times I could observe many nods, and winks, and sly grins pass between the captain and the mate as they occasionally looked towards me; though I sat quietly swallowing my victuals, and appeared not to notice them. After what I had learned from their conversation regarding the law as it referred to negroes in America, I was glad to perceive that the countenance of neither indicated any malignant feeling towards me, and I felt thankful to God that my life was not in danger. Nothing could have been easier than for Winton to have had me thrown overboard some dark night; I considered, therefore, that my case might be much more grievous than it was, and I endeavoured to await calmly and submissively the will of the Almighty.

On the fiftieth day after our departure from Africa,

the captain found by his observations at noon, that we were within a hundred miles of the coast of Carolina, and gave orders to prepare the anchors and cables ready for service. I could observe that the water was beginning to change from the deep blue of the main ocean to a lightish green, and it became more and more so as we got westward. As we were running about eight knots an hour, we had soundings in the afternoon, about six o'clock; and by midnight the Charleston light was visible, like a large star, alternately appearing and disappearing; and the weather being very fine, we kept running on till within a few miles of the lighthouse. The nature of this light interested me very much. Every minute, or so, a bright glare would flash all across the water between the shore and our ship, and then all was pitch darkness for a few seconds; all which seemed very strange to me. I may mention that in the forepart of this day, while yet a hundred miles from shore, the captain and some of the crew said they plainly smelt the scent of the pine woods ashore. The ship was kept under easy sail all night, and soon after daylight we could discern the tops of the trees, which seemed like a low dark line in the horizon; and presently we could discern the white sandy beach with the surf breaking over it. Shortly afterwards a beautiful little sloop came towards us, and sent out a small canoe with three or four men in it; one of whom, as black as myself, came on board, and to my great astonishment and delight, took the command of the ship. Thinks I to myself all will be right now: I shall surely have *one* on my side; but I soon found that this man was only hired to steer the ship for a few miles, and then had no more to do with it. This man's name was Pruivus; he was one of the best pilots belonging to the port; and at last, after serving in this capacity for forty-five years, was drowned in the hurricane of 1822. I was, at all events, much gratified to find one of my countrymen filling a post of such importance. We safely crossed the bar, which is sometimes very dangerous to vessels; it has only thirteen feet or so at low water, and the sea runs very high upon it when the wind is easterly. Soon afterwards we neared Sullivan's Island, a spot where the Carolinians resort to in summer. I was quite astonished at the appearance of the houses, and of a strong fort mounted with heavy cannon; but the strangest sight of all to me, was a number of carriages drawn by horses along the beach. In an hour more we anchored close to the city, which presented a very handsome appearance, and, together with some hundred or two of ships at the wharves, it was a striking sight; yet, as there are very few great buildings in Charleston, and only one very fine steeple, the view fell far short of what I expected to see in the white man's country—I mean, it seemed, to my eyes, nothing at all in comparison to the picture of London in my father's house.

The weather had been warm, and, the day we arrived in Charleston, it was uncommonly hot for that late season of the year; but, next morning, I

H

went on deck before sunrise, and found an amazing change had taken place. During the night the wind had veered round to the north-west, and was blowing keenly; the sky being beautifully clear. I now saw ice for the first time in my life: a skin of ice, about as thick as a dollar, covered small tubs of water on deck. After sunrise, many of the slaves came on deck, but speedily went down again: they could not stand the piercing wind, thinly clad as they were. As the sun gained power, however, it felt comfortably warm. One or two of the negroes took pieces of ice in their hands, to show to their comrades below, who imagined it was glass, until it melted, to their great wonderment.

In the course of the forenoon, the ship was hauled in to a wharf at the north-east side of the city. I saw the captain preparing to go ashore; and, expecting that he would take me with him, I put on some of my finest clothing. When he saw me thus dressed, he said, " Zamba, I think you had better put these clothes off, and just do in the mean time with your ship's clothing. I shall explain to you again about it." I felt hurt at his behaviour: very much disappointed, indeed; for I was, at that time, wofully inexperienced in worldly matters. I imagined that an African king would be regarded with much respect in America; but had I considered a little on some things I had previously heard the captain say, I might have remembered that kings and princes of every description were at a heavy discount in republican America.

The captain came on board in the afternoon; and, soon afterwards, several dray-loads of clothing for the slaves were brought alongside. Next day was still cold; but the whole of the slaves were put ashore, and obliged to wash and scour themselves. They were then provided with tolerably good clothing, made of blue or white coarse woollen cloth, of English manufacture, commonly called "plains." The owners of the ship had provided these; but, had the weather been warm, the poor slaves would have been put up for sale in the scanty clothing they were in. The captain told me they were advertised for sale, which would take place in two days. Meantime we had a considerable number of white gentlemen to visit us, mostly intending purchasers. On the appointed day, the auctioneer, a Mr. Naylor, accompanied by two young clerks, came down; and, after much careful inspection, arranged the whole cargo in separate lots, some of them singly, and others in lots of fifteen or twenty. The single ones were intended for domestic servants in town, and were chosen from the youngest and smartest-looking; the larger lots for the country, or what are called "field hands." At length, a great number of white gentlemen had arrived, and a few white ladies—at least, white women; for their conduct was not such as would entitle them to be called ladies in Europe: in a calm, cool, business-like way, they went around the various groups of negroes, examining and handling their limbs in the same manner as I afterwards saw butchers examining cattle.

The sale soon began, and took up a considerable time; the prices ranging from 250 to 450 dollars a head: the thirty-two negroes whom I had put on board brought nearly 10,000 dollars. It will be thus seen that the owners of the ship had made an excellent speculation: by this trip, as I learned from the captain, they had cleared from 90,000 to 100,000 dollars; and it must be allowed, that great part of this arose from the prudent and humane treatment which was exercised towards the live cargo. No doubt exists in my mind, that the moving principle in all concerned was avarice; and, in this case, it showed that, even from sinister motives, Providence can cause good to be produced at last. In the course of my subsequent experience, I have known ships, of the same tonnage as the *Triton*, arrive from Africa, in which seven hundred and fifty slaves had been embarked; but, owing to cruel usage, scanty and unwholesome provisions, impure air, and absolute filth, which prevailed on board, not more than four hundred lived to reach Charleston; and of these, one-half were in a most weakly and miserable condition, and the remainder could by no means be classed as sound and healthy. In these cases, greed and avarice joined to inhumanity were punished; but at a sad expense of life, as regarded the wretched negroes. I have seen a slave-ship arrive from Africa, in such a condition as to its freight of flesh and blood, that no mortal of ordinary nerves could put his head below the hatch; and in such a miserable state were the negroes, that I have known thirty or forty out of one cargo sent up to the hospital in carts. I heard frequently also, from what I deemed good authority, that on board these crowded and ill-conducted slavers, it was not a rare circumstance for the captain to order such poor slaves as were evidently dying, to be thrown overboard during the night, while yet the pulse of life was beating!

In the evening, when the slaves were sold, the captain, after supper, addressed me as follows:—"You see, Zamba, that, owing to the death of one of the owners of the ship, she is to be sold; and I believe that I shall not continue in the trade at present—I have some arrangements to make in the northern states, which I came from originally; and may, perhaps, settle there altogether; so that you will perceive I cannot go to London with you as I proposed. I will make some bargain for you, however, in Charleston, and will leave you in good hands; and as you have no experience of the world yet, I shall take care of your little property for you in the mean time; and in the course of a few years, when you have learned something, I shall settle accounts with you." "Do you mean to leave me here, sir," said I, "and keep my property also? Surely, captain, after the friendship my father and I have shown you, you cannot be so cruel and dishonourable! If you do, I shall appeal to the white gentlemen in Charleston—I shall tell my whole story to them," said I, rising up from the table, quite indignant. "Sit down quietly, Zamba," said Winton, "and I shall give you a lesson. You see, Mr. Prince," said he, turning to the mate, "how the

African blood gets up. But it is of no use here, Zamba; you must be calm, I tell you, or it will be the worse for you : you will learn before long, my lad, to keep yourself calm and composed like us Yankees. Now, in the first place, you see, Zamba, that, supposing I were to allow you to go into the city of Charleston, and commence your story at the corner of a street, nobody would mind you; or if any one did listen to you for a moment, the white people would call you a lying rascal, and perhaps would beat you, and your own countrymen would only laugh at you. They would say that if you spoke truth you were well served, for that if you brought such a lot of slaves from Africa for sale you well deserved to be sold yourself. In the next place, consider, Zamba, I have given you as much education as will balance your little property; and I shall dispose of you to a good master. Some folks in my place would sell you to a planter in the country to get you out of the way ; and I tell you, Zamba, that if you are not perfectly docile and humble, that I shall do so to-morrow if I choose. You will find the country a miserable place in comparison to the life you may lead with Mr. Naylor; who will instruct you in a clever business and treat you well, provided you conduct yourself properly. And now, Zamba (seeing that I was upon the point of breaking out) if you utter a sentence, I shall take your two trunks from you and all that they contain, and give you a single suit of clothing like to the rest of your countrymen. I have, however, a conscience, Zamba; and you may be truly thankful you have fallen into such good hands: and besides, I am giving you a good moral lesson."

I need not say that I was not altogether thunder-siruck at the captain's behaviour, as I had received some hints previously from his conversations with the mate: but yet it came very hard upon me; although now that I reflect upon it, and know better things, I feel that, on account of my slave trans-actions, I really deserved no sympathy: I was merely reaping the fruits of my labour. Nevertheless, Cap-tain Winton proved himself an unprincipled villain; and he, too, latterly reaped the fruit of his labours. But of this in good time. Thus did this wicked and treacherous captain defraud me of about ten thousand dollars, the price of the slaves; about seven thousand dollars in gold dust, and three thousand in doub-loons, and—what was of more value than all—my liberty! I had no means of redress, none what-ever, even in a Christian country. Neither my word nor my oath would have been of any avail; so in silence and humility was I obliged to submit, and console myself that the rascal had left me my two trunks and their contents.

I went to bed very disconsolate, and dreamed that I was in Africa, with my dear Zillah and my mother, in my own palace, surrounded by my friends and attendants. From this vision of past happiness, never to return, I awoke before sunrise to the sad realities of my condition. At breakfast the captain bantered me about my downcast looks. "Zamba," said he, " you need not take it so much to heart : you will yet think I have been your best friend. Have I not given you a deal of information about the world ? Have I not taught you to read, and brought you to a Christian country, where you will have wise men to teach you all about the Bible, and explain it to you for nothing ? By-and-by you will become a good Christian ; and as for your money, which I am so kind as to take charge of for you, I can assure you, that if left to yourself amongst white people, either here or in Europe, you would not boast of it being your own above ten days : you would be cheated and robbed at every hand. And besides, Zamba, you must know that in a country like this, so much money in the hands of a boy so young as you are would be dangerous—very danger- ous, I tell you. I shall make a bargain to-day with Mr. Naylor for you, and if you are perfectly quiet and respectful, you shall see how much I am inte- rested in you." Thus did this unprincipled man endeavour to cover his avarice and injustice under the cloak of friendship. As I have already hinted, however, my fate might have been much more pitiable.

After dinner the captain came on board with Mr. Naylor and another gentleman. This was the last time I had the honour to sit down to dine with so many white gentlemen ; and from what I have since seen of Carolinian customs, I am at a loss to know how and wherefore it so happened that a negro was so honoured on this occasion. Mr. Nay-

lor was a thin, careful-looking sharp-eyed man; but
there was a benevolent expression in his countenance; and as I had, even at that time, my own
rude ideas of physiognomy, altogether I was pleased
to be in his company. He asked me many questions about African scenery, manners, &c., and I
was very near giving him some answers (as a matter of course) which would reflect discredit on
Captain Winton; but the latter kept a sharp look-
out, and often interrupted and corrected me. The
captain at length said, " Zamba, you will go with
this gentleman, and you will learn to be a clever
man of business in his store. Mr. Naylor is pleased
with your appearance, and the good account I have
given him of you; and I have made a bargain with
him for you. I am to receive six hundred dollars;
which you and I will talk about again: but to convince you and everybody else of my generosity, I
shall return Mr. Naylor three hundred dollars to
be kept for your benefit; and as he is kind enough
to say that he will allow you interest upon it, you
will be able, in the course of a few years, with what
you may otherwise save, to buy your freedom, if
you wish it."

So saying, he took out a purse, counted out
(of my own identical money, I believe) twenty
doubloons, and handed them to Mr. Naylor; who
gave him a receipt for the sum, and at the same
time wrote out on a slip of paper what I afterwards
learned was a promissory-note at ninety days' date,
payable to Captain John Winton, for six hundred

dollars, the same being the price of an African negro named Zamba.

Although I was almost prepared for such treatment, I could not help starting up, and exclaiming—" And is this the way—is this the cruel manner I am to be treated? Have you absolutely sold me as a slave, Captain Winton, after all you have ——" Here I was interrupted by the captain, who also started up, and exclaimed—or rather roared out, for now he was in a dreadful passion—" Hold your tongue, you black rascal, or I'll withdraw my bargain. Just utter one word more, and I shall have you sent to a rice plantation to-morrow, and there they will cool your African blood for you, I can assure you." Mr. Naylor looked at me, as I thought, with much feeling; and as I now saw that it was in vain to contend with fate, I sat down and burst into tears. The gentleman who was along with Mr. Naylor puffed away at a cigar and coolly sipped his wine, muttering to himself, " Curious affair this; can't understand it at all. But, after all, who the devil cares about a nigger?" Mr. Naylor then addressed me, and said, " My boy, you must not take on so. If you conduct yourself properly and honestly, I will take good care of you. I shall send down to-morrow for you." The gentlemen retired soon afterwards, and Captain Winton went ashore with them. When he came back I was in bed, but he came into my state-room, and told me he had a good mind to keep my trunks for my insolence, as he called it, before the white gentlemen. I gave him a meek answer, considering to myself

that " a soft answer turneth away wrath." I slept
little that night, but lay brooding over my unhappy
condition. Yet now I really felt extremely anxious
to be out of sight and out of the power of the
captain.

In the forenoon of next day, one of Mr. Naylor's
clerks, a young Scotchman named Thomson, came to
the ship to bring me away. My trunks were placed
upon a dray, and in a very few minutes I was ready to
go ashore. Just as I was leaving the cabin, the captain, who was busily engaged writing, held out his
hand to me, and said—" Ho! Zamba, don't go away
in that manner without bidding me farewell. I tell
you seriously, that not one slave captain in a thousand would have done for you as I have; and you
may thank your stars that your fate is not worse.
By-the-by, Zamba, though I don't think you will
soon forget me, here is a farewell remembrance to
you—you will, perhaps, be in want of a little pocket-
money." So saying, he gave me a handful of silver
pieces, amongst which were two American gold eagles.
I was inwardly inclined at first to reject it, but
instantly changed my mind, and put the money in
my pocket, though I could not help saying—" Well,
captain, I thank you, although I know it is part of
the price of my own blood."

I then left the ship, and accompanied the young
man who was sent for me; and as I paced across the
wharf, and then along the street, many strange ideas
floated in my brain regarding the inconsistency of
character displayed by this Captain Winton. He

was naturally a warm-hearted, good-humoured man, possessing much information; but avarice, the love of money—that root of all evil—led him to commit the most base and heartless actions. His behaviour towards me was certainly a *moral lesson*, but a dear bought one indeed to me; that is to say, as the world reckons.

On the way to Mr. Naylor's store—he was one of the principal auctioneers in Charleston, and did an immense business—Mr. Thomson, the clerk, entered into conversation with me, and was perfectly astonished to learn that I could read the English Bible tolerably. He seemed very much interested in me; and being quite aware that I was now entirely out of the power of Captain Winton, I told him, in as few words as possible, my whole history, strictly keeping to the truth between man and man. " Well, well, my poor fellow," said he, " I can hardly think you have framed such a story; and if only the one-half of it be true, this Captain Winton for roguery out-Yankees all the Yankees that ever breathed in New England. But you have no redress, my poor fellow; none whatever. However, you have fallen in with a good owner, and if you conduct yourself, as I hope you will, you will not find yourself so uncomfortable as thousands of your countrymen." Oh, how that word *owner* tingled in my ear—it seared my heart like a branding iron. But my conscience told me, in a louder tone than ever, that I deserved my fate. I thanked Mr. Thomson for his encouraging words, and told him that, as a proof of the truth of my history, I could show him some articles in my trunks which would convince him I was correct in my statements.

As we walked along the streets I was much struck with the appearance of the houses; and the shops especially attracted my notice: the wealth which they displayed in goods of every description seemed inexhaustible. But, alas! I was only a poor slave, and in a land of strangers. It cheered me, however, to observe, as I went along, that my countrymen, who thronged the streets at every hand, seemed in general happy and contented. Some were driving drays, others drove fine and elegant carriages, and numbers were busy in the grog stores, or standing in groups at the doors of them; and their incessant laughing and chattering bespoke anything but misery. Then, as we passed the foot of the public markets, the appearance of black men, and women too, decently, and many of them flashily dressed, and all apparently in high spirits, was quite pleasing. As I passed by some barbers' shops I peeped in, and there again were my countrymen quite busy, soaping and shaving the beards, and cutting the hair of white gentlemen.

When we arrived at Queen Street, the lower part of which forms what is called Vendue Range, the clerk ordered the drayman to proceed with my trunks to my master's dwelling-house in Broad Street, and there leave them; he then told me to follow him down the street, in which Mr. Naylor's store was situated. I was quite astonished at the extent of this store, and the way in which it was filled with goods of every description. I thought to myself that there were as many fine prints and handkerchiefs as would supply every woman in Africa, or even in the world, with clothing; and such quantities of beautiful rifle guns, pistols, and swords, were to be seen also, as perfectly amazed me. All these goods were to be sold by auction. My master spoke a few words to me kindly, saying no work would be required of me that day, and I might merely walk about the store, and satisfy my curiosity. Mr. Thomson, also, behaved with much condescension to me: he pointed to various bales and boxes, and seemed gratified that I could tell him, in plain English, the names of the letters marked on them. I was somewhat at a loss to make out figures or numbers; but I attained this knowledge soon afterwards. Mr. Thomson told me he expected I should be very serviceable in the store, and that it would be greatly in my favour if I behaved civilly and respectfully to all, and was always prompt and active. Surliness and slowness, he said, were the besetting faults of my countrymen; "but you were a prince, Zamba," added he, laughing, " and must not lose your character."

In the afternoon, I was taken up to my master's house, which was a large brick building, and, as I afterwards perceived, splendidly furnished. At the back of the house, and on each side of a large court, paved with brick and kept very clean, were situated houses for the servants: very snug two-story wooden buildings. I was allowed to occupy part of an upper room in one of them, into which my trunks were taken; and I was welcomed by two or three of my countrymen (Africans, I mean), and about half a dozen negro women, who were all employed in some way or other about the house. Soon afterwards, we had supper, which was both abundant and agreeable. Some of my fellow-servants belonged originally to my own part of Africa; so that I had many questions to answer in the course of the evening. I was gratified to find that although all of them had a great desire to visit their native Africa for a time, they seemed of opinion that they should like again to return to America. This, however, it must be observed, was only the bright side of slavery; or, at least, the tolerable side of it, if I may say so: and it must, indeed, be a most awful and miserable condition of human nature, which can exhibit nothing save hopeless and helpless misery and despair.

In due time, I went to bed for the first time in the free and generous land of Columbia: so called, at least, by white men in America. Although under a comfortable roof, and upon a snug bed, I could by no means go to sleep. My feelings were various and complicated, and I began to consider whether or not I had great room for self-congratulation. It is true that I had been most wofully duped by Captain Winton; but, on the other hand, as I have already admitted, I deserved it; and, besides, I had yet a considerable amount of property remaining. I argued thus with myself:—" What right had Captain Winton to seize my property, and sell me as a slave?" But then my conscience told me plainly, "What right had you, Zamba, to put on board the *Triton* thirty-two fellow-creatures—nay, fellow-countrymen—and congratulate yourself that you would get rich by selling them in a foreign land?"—"Oh!" says I to myself, "they were either my captives in war, or I paid a fair price for them?"—"Very well, Zamba," said conscience; "but does not common reason teach you,—did not the Holy Book, which you partly understood, tell you clearly—that you should not do that with other men, which you would not wish them to do to you?" Thus I found that all my reasonings with conscience ended in my own conviction; and became quite convinced that I had more reason to be thankful for the mercies and advantages which I still possessed, than cause to murmur at the treatment I had received from Captain Winton. I have often considered since, that as long as a man's conscience speaks to him in loud and decisive tones, he has no occasion to despair. At length I fell asleep, and dreamed again and again of poor Zillah and my mother.

CHAPTER VII.

Zamba in an Auction-store in Charleston—First Sabbath in a Christian Country—Goes to a Presbyterian Church—Description of the Scene, and Reflections thereon—A Negro Acquaintance—A White Friend and Counsellor—Negro Finery and Politeness—Zamba goes to an Episcopal Church—His Account of the Service, and Reflections on the Sermon—Goes to a Methodist Chapel—Effect of the Service on Zamba and his Brethren—The Sermon, and Reflections thereon.

I AROSE at daylight next morning, and found that some of the servants had been up for an hour or two. Mr. Thomson, who lodged with my owner, sent for me, and told me to follow him to the store. When we got there, he made me assist him, and take dry goods out of boxes and bales, and arrange them on shelves, and also do some other light work about the store. He conversed with me a good deal, but only when the other clerks did not observe him ; for they were chiefly American-born, and considered all conversation with a negro, except what business absolutely required, quite derogatory to their dignity as free-born republicans.

I

In a few days, I became tolerably expert in handling goods, and the time passed on pleasantly but
for the thoughts of my own native home. Sunday at
length came; and I shall never forget the first Sabbath I spent in America. It was, I think, the 29th of
November. My master told me I might go to some
church, with some of the other servants; but that
afterwards he would now and then require my services on that, as well as on other days, to wait at
table. He said to me, smiling, " If you get on as
well as I have seen you do for the short time now
past, Zamba, I have no doubt that you will yet be a
free man. It is for your own benefit partly that I
shall have you instructed to be a house, as well as a
store, servant: you will thus learn a good deal of the
world; and if you are particularly civil and serviceable to your superiors, you will now and then be
getting a few dollars."

Mr. Thomson saw me before he went to church,
and told me I might follow him. Although he
seemed much interested about me, and was of a frank
open disposition, he could not avoid participating in
the prejudice which generally prevails in Carolina
against the black race. To have walked *alongside*
of him in public would have been considered an open
breach of the peace; I, therefore, respectfully kept
a few paces in his *wake*. When we arrived at the
church, which was the chief Presbyterian place of
worship in the city, he pointed to a door at the left
hand, and told me to go in there and walk up stairs.
I did so, and found a number of people of my own

colour already seated.   In the opposite gallery were
a number of white people, and the space below was
about half filled with white ladies and gentlemen.
I afterwards learned that in every church in the
city, of whatever denomination, one side of the
gallery is wholly appropriated to the accommodation
of white strangers, and the other side for people of
colour.

This regulation, certainly, indicates genuine good
feeling and real practical Christian charity.   Did
such a spirit pervade all her institutions and customs, America might then hold up her head among
the nations of the earth.

After some time the clergyman entered and read
part of a psalm, as usual in the Presbyterian service; and immediately afterwards about twenty
white men and women in the front of the gallery
commenced singing.   I could not well make out the
words they sang, and asked a man who sat near
me what they meant.   " Hold your tongue, boy,"
said he; " mustn't talk in meeting.   Tell you dey
worship God; so be quiet like good fellow."   I observed that only some of the white people joined in
singing, although the most of them opened a book,
and seemed very serious; but amongst all the black
folks on my side of the church not one book was to
be seen, and of course they did not join in worship-
ping God.

Thinks I to myself this is very strange, but no
doubt the white folks know best what is right; or,
perhaps, they think it would hurt their dignity to

sing with poor slaves. I was rather out in my con-
jectures, as will appear by-and-by.

A prayer was, as usual, then offered up, and I
was pleased to find that the minister prayed for all
men, master and servant, bond and free. The minister then gave out a chapter in the Bible, and commenced reading; again most of the white people
opened their books. I had a Bible in my pocket,
but felt at a loss what to do, from fear of giving
offence; but after a minute's hesitation I took it
out, and with a little difficulty found the place.
Instantly many eyes were turned upon me, especially
those of my own countrymen. I felt very much
abashed, lest I was doing something displeasing to
the white people; but, as Providence would have
it, in the very chapter which the minister was reading, occurred these words, at the very instant I was
in my perplexity, " Search the Scriptures, for in
them ye have the words of eternal life, and they
are they which testify of me." I instantly felt my
spirit refreshed, and thought to myself, " Since the
Almighty hath been pleased that I have acquired
the art of reading, I am not only permitted by Him,
but commanded to search the holy book."

The minister then lectured on Ephesians vi. 5,
" Servants be obedient to your masters, according to
the flesh." He certainly explained very minutely
the duty which servants, especially bondsmen, owed
to their masters and superiors; and held forth
awful denunciations, both in this life and through
all eternity, upon all who dared to step aside from

the path of duty. Said he, " Even though you
should have reason to complain of the hardship of
your case, remember, that ' whom the Lord loveth
he afflicteth, and scourgeth every son he taketh to
himself.' And remember, also, my black friends
(he was very, very careful to avoid calling us brethren),
what holy Paul saith, ' I have learned in whatsoever condition I am to be content.' "

There is no doubt but this clergyman was merely
doing his duty; but I could take notice, even at
this my first experience of a sermon, that he never
once alluded to any duty which mutually belonged to the master towards his dependants and
slaves.

The service ended in the usual manner, and I
returned, well pleased that I would now be in the
way of hearing the Bible explained to me ; and,
above all that, from hearing how the clergyman
addressed *his* brethren, I should soon be enabled
to express my feelings to *my* brethren in a becoming
manner. On coming out of church, the black—an
old grey-headed man—whom I had addressed at
the commencement of the service, came with me
and said, " My boy, I see you is a stranger ; but
how hab you come to read Bible ? Can't suavey
(understand) this!" I explained in a few words how
I had been so favoured. " Ah! well, well, boy, you
may tank God for this. Buckra can't take knowledge to read from you now. But do you hearee me :
in dis fine free country "—(here he looked round for
fear of being overheard)—" you never would have

learn to read good book; white man's law fine any man one hundred pounds who would offer to teach poor black man A B C; and if you, my poor boy, offer to teach any of your comrade one single word to read, you either pay fine or go to jail, and buckra take payment out of your bare back with one good hard cow's skin—dat is white man's law, boy; but, for all dat, some few black folks in Charleston have got knowledge how to read in quiet way, and can write a little too; but all under a cloud you see. Buckra man terribly 'fraid we get too wise," said the old man, with a peculiar grin.

We then parted, but not before I had received an invitation to visit old Jerry and his wife; and we soon afterwards became very friendly.

When I returned to my master's house, I saw Mr. Thomson in the back yard. He asked me to come up to his room, and requested me to read him a chapter in the Bible. I did so, and he was pleased to say that I must have considerable natural abilities, else I could not have made such progress in the cursory manner I had received my lessons. " As I keep my own room a great deal in the evening," said he, "I will run the risk of giving you some lessons myself; and I shall also teach you to write and count. This must be kept very quiet, however, Zamba; for if found out giving you lessons of the kind I shall be heavily fined, and incur the ill-will of many in this place." He then expressed a wish that I should go to an Episcopalian church in the afternoon, and to a Methodist one in the evening. I

should like to know," said he, "which form of
worship, of all you hear this day, interests your feelings most. But remember, Zamba, when you enter
the house of God you must throw away all thoughts
of the world, or of business; and the first thing you
ought to do is to lift up your heart inwardly to God,
and pray that your eyes, and your heart, and your
soul may be opened to the truth; and that you may
be enabled to see that you, as well as all men, are
but poor, perishing, lost sinners: lost beyond all
redemption, if the Holy Spirit conduct you not
to the foot of the cross—even to the Lord Jesus
Christ, who never did, and never will refuse salvation to all such as come unto Him in sincerity,
and with humble and contrite hearts. I hope,
Zamba," said this excellent young man, taking
me by the hand, "that you will yet have reason
to bless the day when you came to this country;
and that you will even look upon Captain Winton as a friend, and pray for him as one who,
in the hands of Providence (although to suit his
own evil purposes) hath been the means of snatching
you as a brand from the fire. I do hope, Zamba,
that even now, in your condition as a slave, you will
be brought from a state of sin and doubt and
darkness, to the marvellous light, and freedom, and
purity of the gospel of the Lord Jesus. I do pray,
as your friend, that you may receive, even here,
a treasure such as the world cannot give, and
(blessed be God!) such as it cannot take away—a
treasure altogether different from, and infinitely more

to be desired than, the few handfuls of gold which a wicked man has deprived you of."

Tears ran down the cheeks of this good young man, as he addressed me; and I felt something inexpressibly delightful within my breast at so much unlooked-for kindness.

It is now nearly forty years since this young and truly sincere disciple of the Lord Jesus exchanged this life of care, and trial, and uncertainty, for an inheritance incorruptible, undefiled, and which will never fade away—at least so is my humble belief and hope; and yet often and again do I behold in my imagination his open and benevolent countenance, as he addressed me, more as if I had been a brother and friend than a poor ignorant bondsman.

In the afternoon I accompanied one of my fellow servants to an Episcopalian church; and on the way thither I could not help being much gratified at the appearance made by my countrymen and countrywomen. Many of the latter were dressed in a very elegant style; which, although it pleased me then, I have long since ceased to admire, being by far too gaudy, and quite unbefitting their station: what with flaming silk shawls, silk stockings, and red-heeled morocco shoes, they seemed prepared for some jollification rather than anything else; and some of them, sporting fine parasols, tripped along the pavement with much levity and frivolity.

It occurred to me, "where have they procured all these fine things? Not in a very creditable way, I fear." I afterwards found this to be true in regard to hundreds of them; and little to the honour and discretion of their white lords and masters. It was a gratifying thing to me, however, to find my country-folks so very agreeable and polite to one another, when they chanced to meet in the street. They invariably addressed each other—with a marvellous deal of bowing and curtseying, and shaking of hands —as daddy and mammy, sister and broder, sir and madam, and received similar salutations in return with great seeming satisfaction; evincing by the loud tones in which they spoke, no habitual dread or terror of their superiors. Many young black men were dressed as finely and fashionably as the first gentlemen in the city; with fine cambric-frilled shirts, and adorned with sparkling jewels, they walked along as proudly as any peacock in the meridian sun. I observed, as I walked very slowly along to see how matters went, one good-looking young black address a couple of young ladies as black as himself. Taking off his glove and kissing his hand, he bowed almost to the ground, and then kept his hat off his head altogether, for some time. " How you do, dear Misses Sarah and Dinah ? I hope I have the pleasure of seeing you this morning in clever good health ; hope mamma, and all friends come on well. Will you allow me the supreme felicity of waiting upon you to church ?"

I also observed in my progress to church, that the doors of a few shops stood open, and that people were buying and selling goods within. I was told these were Jewish traders ; the rest of the shops and stores were all closed and quiet.

We soon arrived at the church, which was very handsome and elegant, and fitted up differently from the one I had attended in the morning. When the organ commenced playing, I was literally thunder-struck with the tremendous and sublime music; so different from anything I had ever heard or imagined. I, however, could make no sense out of the words which were chanted or sung. I could understand some of the prayers, and was much pleased to hear many of the blacks join in this part of the service, as they kneeled down with much decency and apparent seriousness. The service seemed to me, however, to be too complicated for such a simple and unlearned person as myself; and I really conceived that the simple prayers of the Presbyterians came nearer to my view of things. The English mode seemed certainly more calculated to keep the attention of the hearers awake; but if I may dare to express myself, there was too much bustle and stiff formality about it: the other form appeared to come more directly from the heart.

After some time, the clergyman, having retired and again made his appearance in another dress, which was a new matter of wonder to me, gave out the text,—" Believe on the Lord Jesus Christ, and thou shalt be saved." He went on to explain his text, and I thought to myself that many of his re-marks particularly applied to my own situation. He gave a short sketch of the history of man from his creation—of his speedy and fatal fall from innocence and consequent happiness—and of the natural enmity

of his heart to all that was good. He then expa-
tiated upon the necessity for a Saviour, and showed
that such could not be found either in one of the race
of fallen mankind, or even of the more exalted angels
of heaven ; who, high as they were, stood charged
with folly in the eyes of Him who is altogether purity
and perfection. It was requisite, then, that one
should be found altogether spotless and pure, and free
from the taint of sin in any degree—who could lay
his hand upon fallen, wretched, and forlorn man, on
the one side, and upon a justly offended and infinitely
holy God, upon the other, and reconcile the one to
the other. " An intercessor," said he, " must be
found, who, by his own obedience and suffering, as a
spotless and sinless being, can atone to infinite justice in a satisfactory manner for the sins and rebel-
lions of the millions of lost mankind. And such a
mediator could only be found in the person of Jesus ;
who, although dwelling in the bosom of the Father
from all eternity, of his own free will and benevolence
towards mankind, became, in due time, a sacrifice,
and, by the shedding of his precious blood upon the
cross, made an end of sin, and finished transgression
He then gave a brief view of the life, character, and
doings of the Saviour whilst upon earth. " Would
it," continued he, " ever have entered into the imagination of man or angel, that He who was the Second
Person in the Godhead, and who thought it no rob-
bery to be equal with God, should assume the form
and submit to the inconveniences and infirmities
attendant upon the sons of men—that he should lead

a life of humiliation, and at last lay down his life for a wretched and rebellious race? Such sublime and godlike ideas could only have emanated from a source exalted infinitely above all that created intelligence could ever imagine; and the conduct of the blessed Saviour whilst amongst men was so transcendantly pure and benevolent, so superior to anything that had hitherto been seen upon the earth, that even his bitterest enemies found that it was altogether absurd to deny the supernatural effects produced by his mere words. When they saw the lame and the blind, who had been so from their mother's womb, at once restored to sight and hearing, and when, even before many witnesses, the dead were called forth from their graves; still, in the malignity and obstinacy of their hearts, they refused to receive the light into their darkened minds, and, since they could not deny the plain and open fact that such miracles were performed, attributed the power of the blessed Saviour to magic and the agency of evil spirits. Before our Saviour's time," continued he, " it had been said by wise and sober men and learned philosophers, that men should act as they would that others should do to them; but it was reserved for the Saviour himself to teach mankind a doctrine hitherto unthought of, and altogether in itself bespeaking its high origin — namely, that we should forgive our enemies, do good to those who despitefully use us, and pray for those who revile and persecute us; in a word, that we should return good for evil. And now, my friends, believe in this Jesus, and you shall be saved. But it is not a mere simple assent to the truth as a matter of historical fact that will save you. Believing, you must *act*, and show, by your conduct towards all men and towards your Creator, that you believe the Lord Jesus to be his only and well-beloved Son ; and as an evidence that your belief is genuine, you will endeavour literally to follow Jesus in all your words and actions, and even in your very thoughts. In one word, remember that the Lord Jesus expressly said, ' If you love me, you will keep my commandments.' And, again, ' Why call ye me, Lord, Lord, and do not the things that I say ?' "

Pardon me, gentle reader, for being so diffuse upon the matters of my first Sabbath-day's experience in a Christian land. I am aware that some who may honour me by a perusal of these papers will slip over what they may deem cant and hypocrisy ; but I am also aware that there are others who will feel interested in tracing my progress from darkness to light, and from the power of Satan to the glorious liberty of the sons of God.

On my way home from church, I reflected thus to myself : " Surely these white people ought to be very good and happy, possessing so many advantages and blessings. What splendid and substantial houses, and what elegant furniture ! Such fine clothing to wear—such luxurious food and wines to eat and drink—such fine streets to walk in—such elegant carriages to ride in—and, above all, such noble houses in which to worship God ! And what sublime music to elevate and soothe their feelings ! But, ah ! why should they be so unjust towards the black people? Why, above all things, debar them from learning to read and write, and thus, in a great measure, cause God's own message from heaven to be a sealed book to those who, from their ignorance, stand most in want of it?"

I felt greatly comforted by what I had heard this day, and bethought myself that I should now—at least once in seven days—experience a delight which nothing else on earth could give me. Is it not, surely, a high honour for sinful and rebellious man to be allowed to lay his heart open before God — to implore his assistance and his advice—and to hold communion with him, so to speak, as a friend and a councillor? I, however, learned from my comrade that there were thousands of white people, and also many blacks, in Charleston, who never entered a church door from year to year; choosing rather to go upon pleasure-parties into the country, or even, still worse, to spend the whole of the Lord's holy day in drinking, gambling, quarrelling, and blaspheming in public houses. How often, alas! do men, in all countries and stations, look upon God's choicest blessings with an apathy and an indifference alike strange and lamentable! Because they have, all their life long, been accustomed to find them within their reach at any time and at all times, they think them too common and familiar to be much cared for.

In the evening, my comrade went with me to a Methodist chapel. He told me the black people chiefly joined this sect of Christians. They seemed generally to have more sympathy with our race, and did not assume so much state and superiority as other sects.

Soon after we entered the meeting, a hymn was read; the person who led the singing slowly repeated line after line, and, to my great satisfaction, he was instantly joined by the whole of the congregation, white and black. Many of the latter—especially the females—appeared to understand the music well, and sung with beautifully clear voices. I attempted to follow, to the best of my ability, and felt within me a species of happiness hitherto unknown. I felt that, in this the first audible offering of my heart to Almighty God, I was now and for ever bursting the chains of ignorance and paganism, and that henceforth I should consider myself as enlisted under the banner of our Lord Jesus.

The prayer which immediately followed appeared to be indeed a prayer from the inmost parts of the soul. It was spirit communing with spirit. The speaker seemed to be deeply impressed with the idea that he was in the presence of an omnipotent and awful Being, altogether full of goodness and mercy— a Being whom the heaven of heavens cannot contain, and who yet deigns to dwell in the heart of the humble and contrite man. As the speaker went on (and I took notice that he, as well as many of the congregation, kneeled at the commencement of the prayer), he entered more and more into the spirit of his holy exercise; again and again he clasped his hands with energy, and called, in a voice still louder and louder, upon the Lord, to look down and have mercy upon all present. Many of the white audience seemed equally earnest, and called aloud, with all the fervour of an aroused spirit, for mercy and peace. Many, too, of the blacks—especially the females—appeared to be greatly moved and excited, and even lost all command over their feelings, beating their breasts, and calling out—" Lord, have mercy upon us sinners!"

I am quite aware, from my subsequent experiences, that the Methodists have been accused of an improper degree of fanaticism and enthusiasm, according to the notions of worldly men. No doubt, there are sometimes extravagances committed in the Methodist mode of worship; but is there no allowance to be made for simple and unlearned people, who, perhaps for the first time in their lives, have their eyes opened, as it were, in an instant, by the power of the Holy Spirit, which oftentimes pierceth as a sword, separating the joints and marrow? In the days of our Saviour, there is no doubt that, on the impulse of the moment, many sinners called aloud, in the streets and in the fields, for mercy; and there is as little doubt that the men of the world in those days looked upon them also as mad enthusiasts.

On my way home from church, I began to question myself, whether I considered any worldly disadvantages and disappointments I had experienced, were to be compared with the advantages I now enjoyed?—hearing the gospel preached to me, as it were, and the infinite love and salvation of Jesus offered to me, a poor miserable and ignorant sinner; and I further asked myself, "Are you perfectly at peace in your heart with Captain Winton, and can you fall down on your knees and pray for him, and forgive him from the bottom of your heart?" I will candidly own that this latter part of the matter seemed not altogether so clear to me as my conscience told me it should be. As I thought further of it, however, I was, by the holy Spirit of God illuminating my heart and eyes, brought so far, that before I slept that night I fell upon my knees, and offered up a prayer, entreating God that he would *enable* me to forgive Captain Winton *soon*. But in the midst of my devotion conscience again interposed, and whispered, "But, Zamba, what if God removes you from this world before daylight; how will you dare to stand before Him, and your enemy still unforgiven?" I found there was no tampering with conscience; so at once I petitioned, "Lord, enable me this moment to forgive my enemies, wherever or whoever they may be; or enable me altogether to forget them."

The serious reader will perceive what struggles still went on within me betwixt the natural heart of sin and corruption, and the holy influences of the blessed Spirit. It is sometimes very difficult to drive the old man utterly away from the sinful heart, which he has so long occupied: he will often assume a less revolting shape, and attempt to go halves with the struggling sinner; blinding him so far that he thinks he has wholly obtained the triumph over sin,

K

when he is yet but in the hottest of the battle. The young man with whom Jesus communed regarding his previous life and character, made a stand at the sacrifice proposed by Christ: for the sake of his worldly possessions, which were great, he turned his back upon the precious jewels which Christ had in store for him; and, as many others since have done, and even now still do, went away—away to enjoy, for a few fleeting years or days, the gross pleasures of the senses; and for ever to forego those pleasures which are at God's right hand.

CHAPTER VIII.

Captain Winton visits the store of Zamba's master—Zamba finds a
friend and teacher—Puts his money to interest—Effects of the
American War—Negro Slavery in Charleston—Auction Sales of
Negroes—The Cowskin—Horrors of a Slave-ship—Affecting scene
—Price of Slaves—Captain Pompey—Emancipation prohibited.

NEXT morning I resumed my duties at the store, and
soon became tolerably expert at handling and arranging goods.

In my different conversations with Mr. Thomson,
I had given him a history of the manner in which
Captain Winton had behaved towards me; and, as a
matter of course, Mr. T. had made no secret of it,
so that the other clerks, and many customers who
frequented the store, were acquainted with it. It
is well known to the world that the Americans are a
very inquisitive race; and I am aware, from my own
experience, that they do not let any story they get
hold of lose anything in its travels. I excited much
more interest in the concern than was altogether
agreeable; for the fact of the matter was, that
although all joined in condemning the Captain to a

K 2

certain extent, the laugh was invariably turned
against me at the last: I was told half a dozen
times every day, by some one or other, although
in a good-humoured way, that I was well served.
" Really, you were a fine fellow, Zamba, to be in
the way of selling thirty-two of your own countrymen.
Dog should not eat dog, Zamba."

Captain Winton had been several times at the
store regarding business with my master; but as yet
I had never encountered him closely: he generally
came round by a back way, which led to the counting-
house. Whether it was really the case or not, may be
doubtful, but I could not help imagining that he
did not wish to see me: to face me, I would say, eye
to eye: such cowards does guilt cause men to be.
As chance would have it, however, one afternoon
Captain Winton, with another gentleman, came
walking down the front pavement, and were passing
the large open door, around and within which were
about a score of dealers (Jews, Gentiles, and all sorts),
waiting to receive the goods they had purchased in
the forenoon. One of these, a New England man,
and a very merry fellow, called out, " Ho! Winton,
come hither and tell us all about the story of the
Black Prince," at the same time pointing to me as I
was engaged in handing out goods. The Captain
did not change colour, but he looked rather black, as
I have heard people say, and answered, " What do
you mean now, Bennet? You are always upon some
nonsense or other." " Why, I guess anyhow, Captain,
it was no nonsense of you to make twenty thousand

particular hard dollars at a slap ; and all without any
trouble, too, as they tell me, excepting a lesson or
two in the primer to this poor black Nincompoop.
I must acknowledge, Winton, you do credit to old
Connecticut—you have beat all to particular smash
your cousin Ezekiel, who sold some barrels of wooden
nutmegs last year here at Vendue.   Ha ! ha!
Winton, you are a real king of trumps, and don't
do things by halves.   But, I say, Winton, for old
times you must stand treat the next time you come
up my way in King Street."   All this was said in
a free and easy sort of way ; nevertheless, it evidently
went to the quick; as, however well-pleased people
may feel with themselves at making a spec in a
way of this kind, they do not wish the world to
know all the particulars.   The laugh completely
turned against the Captain for once ; and a
good-natured shopkeeper, who had once or twice
before spoken to me kindly, slipt a quarter dollar
into my hand, as I assisted him to put his goods
upon a dray, saying, " Never mind, Zamba, you
are a clever fellow, and will be a man yet.   And as
for that rascally Captain, I tell you, as sure 's my
name is Tobias, your money won't thrive long with
him : he is too fond of the dice-box."

I must confess that I felt a secret satisfaction in
seeing Winton thus annoyed.   This, then, was a
pretty sure sign that my heart was yet in the gall
of bitterness.   I consoled myself, however—and how
glad are all men to catch at a straw in extremity—
that I was on the way to better things.   I went

home in the evening and had my supper. And I
may here remark that, to use a common saying,
I and the rest of my fellow servants were fed like
princes; and the large kitchen, with its fire blazing
every evening, and its well-furnished table, was by
no means a scene of gloom or discontent. I was
often, indeed, at a loss to know why we were
permitted to be so merry and cheerful. But, as I
shall yet show, there was an amazing and awful
difference between our situation and that of thousands
of our countrymen.

After supper, Mr. Thomson sent for me to his
room. He was desirous to know what were my feelings in regard to the good things I had heard on the
Sabbath, and which of the churches I should prefer
going to regularly. I at once told him, that I preferred the Methodists; "because," said I, "they
seem to address their sermons very particularly to
the blacks; and they seem pleased to hear us join in
singing and praying. And, besides all this, I think
they are a very plain and simple people, and more
adapted than the other sects to teach us poor blacks."
"I believe you are not far wrong, Zamba," said he.
"You may go and hear a few of the other sects which
are in the city; but the sooner you fix upon one, the
better. Keep by one minister: you are not so likely,
in that case, to be tossed about by every wind that
blows."

Although I had made up my mind, after Captain
Winton's affair, to put my trust in no white man, I
was now inclined to alter my mind. Mr. Thomson

seemed such an amiable young man, and appeared
to have my soul's interest so much at heart, that I
thought I could not do better than consult and con-
fide in him in temporal affairs.

I told him about the gold I had contrived to save
from the Captain's clutches, and how it happened.
He was quite delighted to learn that I had shown
so much prudence and forethought, and said that it
would be a great pity to let my money lie idle in a
trunk.   He said that Mr. Naylor was a very rich
man, and a most honourable man; but that people
in business were never the worse for having plenty of
ready money.   He would speak to Mr. Naylor on the
subject, and had no doubt but that he would readily
take charge of my little stock, and give me good
interest for it.   " In the mean time, Zamba," said he,
" although you have far more money than would purchase your liberty at a fair price, I would, as a friend,
advise you to remain as you are ; you could not be
more comfortable anywhere than in Mr. Naylor's
service ; and you will be the better for more experience before you venture on the world on your own
account.   I suppose, Zamba," said he, smiling, " you
will be often thinking of home, and your wife and
mother ; but just be patient a little, there is no
saying what the Almighty will bring round for you.
And let me tell you, Zamba, that, although I do not
say much about it, I think as often about the hills of
my own dear Scotland, as you can do about Africa ;
and I have a dear father and mother there, too ; and
sisters and brothers, whom I dream of almost every

night." He then told me that his father was a clergyman in Scotland, with a small income and a large
family; and that, as he himself was very saving in
his habits, and had a good salary besides his board,
he was enabled to send his father every year, about
two hundred dollars; "which is," said he, "not
near so much as some of my fellow-clerks annually
spend on theatre tickets, cigars, and brandy. It is
to my virtuous parents, however, and the grace of
God, that I owe all; and I must not boast of my
virtue: my comrades lay out their money to please
themselves, and so do I."

The next morning early I opened my hidden treasures, and it was found that I had about five pounds
of gold dust; this was afterwards sold at 250 dollars
per pound, making 1250 dollars; and the thirty doubloons came to 450 dollars, so that I had 1700 dollars
to place in the hands of Mr. Naylor, who congra-
tulated me on my prudent conduct. " I will allow
you," said he, "at the rate of seven per cent., Zamba;
so that you will have 119 dollars every year coming to
you as interest; and it will always be increasing. And
now I tell you, in the presence of Mr. Thomson, that
in case of my death, I shall give you a letter declaring
you a free man, and will also give you a receipt for
the money; for you must understand that, by the laws
of this State, a slave cannot own property in his own
right. You will draw out these papers, Mr. Thomson,
and we shall show poor Zamba, that all white men
are not exactly so greedy as Captain Winton." I was
much struck at my master's condescension, and very

much amazed to find that money *grew* so fast, from year to year, in the hands of white men.

Excepting anxious thoughts regarding Africa and my dear friends there, my mind and body, I may say, were in a sound and comfortable state. Mr. Thomson faithfully performed towards me the part of a teacher: giving me lessons, at least four times in the week, in reading or writing, not forgetting arithmetic; and he was pleased to say that I was a most hopeful scholar. He used to say, "How blind are the rulers of this State to debar black men from the knowledge of letters, and how much are they combating against their own interests: they might have excellent clerks and bookkeepers, without being required to pay high salaries to white men. For instance, now, Zamba, I make no doubt but that, with proper instructors, and having the thing done openly, in a few years you would be as expert at writing and figures as many clerks in Charleston, who receive 1000 or 1200 dollars per annum. But prejudice, stupid prejudice, will often blind men to their dearest interests; and the dearest interest of man in America seems to be the acquisition of dollars and cents: there are merchants in this city, who, by educating their own negroes, might save annually from 6000 to 8000 dollars." For my own part, I found that the more I read in books, the more was I inclined to read on and know as much as possible regarding the people of other countries; and I found that the little learning I had already obtained was of great service to me, in performing my duty towards my master.

I may mention, that Mr. Naylor had a most extensive business going on. He sold a vast deal of what is called real property : houses, lands, &c.; also immense lots of goods alongside of ships; lots of negroes, almost every day ; and an immense quantity of dry goods at the store.

Whilst in Mr. Naylor's service, I saw many ups and downs in the commercial world. During the war with Britain, from 1812 to 1815, business was almost wholly at a stand. Let the Americans boast as they will, to use the expression of an old Scotch merchant, who went much about our store : " Anither half year, my braw lads, would finish you, stoup and roup : ye wad be rinnin' red naked, an' no a bowl or a plate, or a hale jug in a' yer aught."

War, in fact, a ruin and a curse to any country, is especially so to America. Her trade was completely knocked up ; and even her agriculture in a great measure : for example, good cotton was offered in Charleston at five or six cents per pound ; but no one would venture to buy it, because they were in daily dread that the British would come in and burn the city and its contents. I recollect, however, a certain Dutch gentleman—who was very wealthy, and had perhaps better information from Europe than some of his neighbours—who ventured upon ten or twelve thousand bales of cotton, at six cents or so, and took his chance of the burning. When peace came, he realized from twenty to twenty-five cents for his whole stock ; thus clearing more than half a million of dollars. I recollect also that the ear-

liest arrivals of goods from Britain brought enormous
prices: blue-edged common dinner plates, which cost
about two shillings per dozen in Liverpool, brought
six dollars, or about twenty-seven shillings. I saw
the same kind, however, sold, in about a twelve-
month afterwards, at half a dollar per dozen: the
market getting overstocked, and sales by auction
being resorted to. Other kinds of goods—British,
French, and German, were equally in demand at the
opening of the trade; but the market was so soon
overwhelmed, that I have seen such sacrifices at
auctions as would cause a man of a mercantile turn
to shed tears.

I had, as yet, in regard to my fellow-countrymen,
observed few of the evils of slavery. Draymen,
porters, and workmen of every description, seemed
generally merry and hearty; and, in the loading of
ships with cotton, rice, &c., a stranger would think
the negro one of the merriest creatures in the world:
such continual singing and bawling going on, as if
there were no such thing as care in the world. But,
as I have already said, I had yet only seen the bright
side of the picture.

To be sure, the very action of exposing my fellows
to sale was a deplorable matter; but to this traffic I
had been habituated, and, I fear that I must add,
hardened. We had almost daily sales of negroes.
But I must particularize a little. When my master
had orders from any customer, for instance, to sell a
single negro, or a few, it was generally called a Lot,
and the sale took place before the Auction Store.

When the number amounted to any thing considerable, they went by the name of a *Gang ;* and the sale took place at the Exchange.

In selling them at the Store, a large table was placed before the door, upon the wooden pavement; and upon this table my master, or one of his partners, mounted, with a paper in his hand and a small wooden mallet. The negro or negroes, generally dressed in their best, were then placed also upon the table, and were told to hold up their heads. Mr. Naylor, or his partner, then read out their description and character : *sound, sober, honest,* and no *runaway,* being almost always part of the latter ; and then the Terms of Sale were stated : cash, or an endorsed approved note, at sixty or ninety days, or sometimes six months.

In the mean time, intending purchasers, including oft-times white ladies, had gathered around the table. Questions were then put to the piece of *living merchandize,* and, in general, quiet and humble answers given; although I have seen some of my race very sullen and refractory. On the other hand, I have seen some young fellows as merry as crickets, laughing and joking with all around. These generally, however, I am aware, could pretty well guess into whose hands they would most likely fall. I have more than once heard a young lad bawl out to a gentleman passing down the Vendue-street : " Do, Massa Robertson, come here, and bid for me, and disappoint old Mr. Lamp, who wants much to have me ; but I would rather sarve you, Sar."

I have, however, witnessed scenes at auctions which

were truly harrowing to the soul; especially in the case of females. I have seen poor women so much agitated, and rending the air so with their screams, that the auctioneer, notwithstanding all his bland-ishments, was obliged to put off the sale till a succeeding day; and the poor women had to be taken into the Store, and revived (for more than once have I seen them faint) with a glass of wine.

What would ladies in civilized and Christian Eng-land think of the FAIR and gentle ladies of free and Christian America—to see, I say, these lilies of the creation at an auction table, putting questions to victims of their own sex, such as no modest *man* would repeat, and that, too, in the presence of a crowd of men? I have seen at the same time men ordering these poor black women to pull down their stockings, and stretching forth their un-hallowed hands to assist the poor creatures in doing so. This was done, as I was told, to ascertain whether the individuals offered for sale, were troubled with diseased or ulcerated legs: but it was done with the utmost coolness; just in the same manner as a butcher handles his four-legged victims.

To recount the strange, cruel, unnatural, and in some few cases humorous, scenes at the sale of negroes which came under my observation, would be endless. I must sometimes adhere to *generals* and not to *particulars*. I may observe, however, that upon an average, the owners of their fellow-men, who thus outraged the first principles of human nature, by making merchandise (and that too in such a glaring manner) of "man, the image of God," even although clothed in a sable skin, generally so arranged matters beforehand, that husband was not separated from wife, father or mother from their children, or children of the same parents from one another.   If they could as well be sold in *lots* conveniently to the purchaser, so far all was good.   If not—that is to say, if the purchaser had not cash, or credit sufficient to go a certain length, or if he required, perhaps, only a female domestic servant—he, without compunction, bought the wife or daughter, and left the husband or father to some other bidder; who, perhaps, lived in a part of the country where there would be no chance of the poor slaves ever again meeting with each other.

I have seen the husband and wife, and sometimes an infant or two, upon the auction table ; the husband with his arms around the neck of his faithful and long-loved, although black partner, imploring, in the most moving language, while the tears trickled down his sable cheeks, that they would not separate him from all that he cared for upon earth ; and the poor woman equally moved, and in many cases more so, beseeching, with all the eloquence of nature's own giving, that she might be allowed to toil the remainder of her earthly existence with the only one her heart ever loved.   But all in vain !   For the convenience of some proud, arrogant, and overbearing planter, or some iron-hearted slave-dealer, who had all his life been accustomed to regard the black race as merely a superior order of brutes, the most sacred and tender links of humanity were torn asunder, and a few coarse jeers and remarks made upon the mighty fuss about nothing. I have heard it remarked a hundred times, " Feelings of a negro! where the devil did they find feelings? No, no, my good fellow (addressing the wretched and broken-hearted husband), your wife and children go with me; she is an excellent cook and laundress I hear, and really I am not in want of a fellow like you at present:" or, " why, really I would go out of my way a few dollars to accommodate you all; but I know well enough that you will soon find a wife, go wherever you may; and as for your wife you seem so uneasy to part with, why, I promise you, I shall find her a husband to her heart's content."

Amongst many of the white people the impression is that a negro has no feelings, although even these know well to the contrary, and merely entertain this idea before the world, to cloak their own want of feeling. I have seen husband and wife so loth to part, that at length the husband was forced into the auction store and compelled to await the arrival of his purchaser, whilst the weeping wife and children were conveyed up the street to a waggon in waiting for them; their lordly, noble, high-souled and generous republican master, bringing up the rear with a cowskin in his hand, applying it now and then, in a gentle way, to the back of his new-made purchase.

And here, by the way, I may let the British reader know what a cowskin is. Many hundred bundles of them have gone through my hands in attending my duty in my master's store. Large quantities came down from the manufactories in the northern States, by almost every ship: for, although these states disown the *holding* of slaves, they have no objection, for the sake of a few dollars in the way of honest trade, as they call it, to supply the southern tyrants with proper instruments of torture.

The cowskin, then, is formed of untanned cow or ox hide, cut in narrow strips, and twisted together in a spiral form, as thick as a stout walkingstick at the butt end, and tapering gradually to a point; and, lastly, coated over with oil paint, generally green. The fact is, that the greater part of them are used as riding-whips. They are so tough and so hard that any person of ordinary strength can leave a deep mark in a *deal board* by one blow of this instrument. It may then be imagined with what effect it tells upon the bare back or legs of a poor negro, or (as happens often enough) a negress.

My master had often the sale of whole cargoes of slaves, " fresh from Africa,"—or, as it turned out in many cases, anything but *fresh*. I have seen ships arrive from my native land with cargoes at least three to one more numerous than that of the vessel in which I myself came to America. The filth and the abomination which some of these presented was perfectly indescribable; and the squalid, wasted, and miserable plight in which the poor negroes or *cargo* appeared, was enough to have checked for ever such traffic, had not the individuals who were embarked in it

been destitute of every feeling which can confer
honour or dignity on human nature. Some of these
poor victims to the white man's love of gold, were so
far gone that I have known the owners of the ship to
murmur and grumble very much at being obliged to
pay duty (which the law compelled them to do) on im-
porting negroes, viz. ten dollars each. "Ten dollars!"
I have heard them say, "why some of these poor
devils are not worth ten cents. But we can't "——
this sentence was left unfinished : they meant, " we
can't well now throw them into the sea, and so evade
the ten dollars; no, that would be *rather* too open,
even for Carolina." But I am quite aware that the
captain was, in some cases, given to understand,
in as delicate a manner as possible, that he should
get rid of such encumbrances on the *east side* of
Charleston bar: that is, somewhere or other in the
bosom of the broad Atlantic.

Slave ships from Africa generally moored off a
place in the north-east side of the city, called
Gadsden's wharf. It was out of the bustle of the
harbour; and here a number of low wooden sheds
or huts were erected, for the accommodation of
imported negroes.

During the warm season, the poor creatures were
landed, and after being washed and cleaned, were
put up for sale, in general with no more than a
yard or two of Osnaburgh round the middle; but in
winter the owners were, for their own sakes, obliged
to furnish them with a few warm clothes, otherwise they would have lost them altogether. The

L

keen sharp air which prevails during some days of the winter months would speedily have finished them.

Although certain that they had come to a country where they would be treated as slaves, and subjected to hard work and hard treatment, without the smallest chance of ever again seeing their native land, yet the negroes upon coming ashore, and being allowed to stretch their limbs, and walk about a little—to refresh themselves in the salt water, and breathe the pure air of heaven — and, above all, being furnished with fresh provisions, it was astonishing to observe how their spirits revived : a change for the better appeared in their countenances, and they expressed their delight, by capering and singing. But no wonder, after all, when we consider the difference between the hold of a ship, containing four or five hundred negroes, surrounded with filth, and suffering from suffocation, and the fresh and grateful free air of heaven.

I would here observe, that in the preceding portion of my narrative, and also in that which is to follow, I have never had recourse to falsehood, in expressing what I have seen or heard ; the case does not require it ; the plain and simple truth will do more for the cause of the black man, than ten volumes of varnished fables : yea, one simple fact, related as it actually happened, will do more for our cause, than fifty exaggerated fabrications. To do justice, then, to the white man, I observed, that in dividing the negroes into *lots* for sale, the captain and mates were always consulted by the owners, and such of the slaves as it could be made out were related to one another, were put in the same lot. I remember one case, however, which created some sensation, even among the hardened slave-dealers.

By some oversight or mistake, a mother was put in one lot, and her only daughter, a fine girl of sixteen or seventeen in another, and when, after the sale, the purchasers were driving away their *lots*, (for, indeed, they were actually *driven* away, like four-footed beasts) the poor girl ran to her mother, and taking her by the hand, was proceeding up the wharf with her. But in a moment, this was discovered by the person who had purchased the girl—for a *particular* purpose, as it afterwards appeared. He instantly followed and seized the girl by the wrist, and although she could not speak a word of English, she manifested by her looks and voice, that she was not deficient in nature's eloquence. She threw her arms around the neck of her mother, who seemed equally moved; and it was not without much difficulty, and many hard blows of the cowskin, that they could be separated. Mr. Naylor here humanely interfered, and endeavoured to effect a compromise or bargain betwixt the planter who purchased the mother, and who resided 150 miles up the country, and the person who had purchased the daughter; but all to no effect. The latter, who resided within 20 miles of Charleston, would hearken to no terms; he had a *particular purpose*, as I have already said, for the girl, and would yield her up to no one.

What this purpose was, I might leave the reader to guess; but as some readers may not be quite conversant with the humane and christian-like laws and habits of Carolina, I may tell him that the poor girl was intended to grace the *harem* of this noble-minded and free-souled republican—*nolens volens*, I may add.

Perhaps the reader may exclaim to himself here, "What do you know about Latin, my black friend?" Why, sir, my kind friend Mr. Thomson, besides instructing me in English, writing, arithmetic, and a little geography, lent me a Latin dictionary, to shew me the derivation of words, and taught me how to use it; so that I have picked up even a little of that ancient and sublime language.

And, by the way, I may mention that during my residence in Charleston, I have been acquainted with negroes and mulattoes, not a few, who could both speak and write in English, French, Spanish, and German.

It is an easy matter for republicans—liberal-minded legislators—to make laws prohibiting the black man from using the means of instruction; but it would be as easy to stay the gulf-stream in its course, as to put these laws in force to the letter. One black man, who possesses a little knowledge, may communicate the same to hundreds of his race, without the cognizance of white men; and there is much more of this going on in Charleston, even now, than the public are aware of. And shall it all come to nought? No! the light, feeble though it be at present, and necessarily communicated amid gloom and privacy, will yet burst forth like a blazing comet, and astonish those despots, who attempt to smother the heavenly spark of knowledge, and to stifle that eager desire for information which exists in the soul of many black men—and black women too.

I hope the kind reader will pardon my frequent digressions; I am not used to book-making, and have no regular plan laid down for my narrative. I write down just as my memory serves me, and from the impulse of the moment. I must also crave pardon for such frequent allusion to self; but I can hardly avoid this piece of egotism.

It may not be out of place here to speak of the price or value of slaves at different periods. From the time of my arrival in America, up till 1807, an immense quantity was imported from Africa. In 1807 the American government nominally abolished the slave trade. I say *nominally*, for although after that year there was no *direct* importation, it cannot be denied that up to this very hour thousands of negroes are annually smuggled into the southern states—especially to the ports in the Gulf of Mexico—from Cuba and the Brazils; and it is also believed, not a few direct from Africa, in an underhand way.

The price of negroes usually varies with the price of rice and cotton; although this rule does not always hold. At this present moment, for instance, while cotton sells at from 6 to 8 cents per pound, a good field hand will bring from 400 to 600 dollars; and I remember well that, in 1817 and 1818, when the same kind of cotton was at its very highest : namely, 33 and 35 cents, the same negro would not have brought above 800 dollars.—I believe, however, that the present high price is maintained on account of the great demand in the far western states ; especially for the newly admitted state of Texas.

The slave-dealers are exulting at this great acquisition at present ; as being, in their opinion, a deadly blow at the abolitionists. Time will, perhaps, yet show that they are in the wrong. Providence sometimes blinds the wicked to their own destruction.

In regard, however, to the price of negroes, I have seen two old women sold for 60 dollars. They were above 80 years of age, and could be of no use as domestics ; unless perhaps to kindle a fire, or watch a pot boiling. In the particular case to which I allude they were purchased by a charitable man, who had some bowels of compassion even for negroes. And it must be remembered here that the owner of slaves cannot, when his negroes get old and feeble turn them into the street altogether : no, he must maintain them in some way, however stinted. The law in this case is not destitute of wisdom and humanity. I may say then, that I have seen negroes sold at all prices, from 30 dollars (6l. 15s. sterling) up to 1550 dollars, (348l. 15s.). I have seen this latter sum paid for a young man of 25, who was a first rate cooper and blacksmith. It will be seen then, from this, that the white man in his capacity of slave-owner, does not enjoy his privileges altogether without some serious drawbacks. The man, for instance, who to-day pays

1500 dollars for a negro, may lose him to-morrow by the unceremonious visitation of that great and invisible power before which all men, bond and free, prince and peasant, must bow, sooner or later.   Or the new made purchase may take it into his head to run away to the woods, or perhaps feign sickness, or, as it has happened more than once, may commit suicide.   Such accidents as these must detract a great deal from the slave-holder's peace of mind.

I mentioned already that I had seen some rather humorous scenes even at the sale of negroes; I shall describe one which took place about six years after my arrival in Charleston.   My master had orders to sell a schooner and her crew; and, accompanied by Mr. Thomson and myself, he proceeded to the wharf (it was Crafts' wharf, I recollect) on the day of sale. After a number of intending purchasers had collected on the schooner's deck and on the wharf, Mr. Naylor read out the particulars of sale, viz. :—"The schooner *Susannah*, with all her apparel and appurtenances, 65 tons register, 3 years old, a regular trader to Georgetown, and carries a large cargo to her tonnage.   Conditions :—an approved indorsed note, at 90 days, with security on the vessel."   Well, the vessel was knocked down at 2250 dollars to a Mr. Lawson.   Mr. Naylor then read on : " Pompey, the Padroon, a black man aged 28, a prime negro—" Here Mr. Naylor was interrupted by Pompey, who stood close beside him on the quarter-deck, rigged out in his best : and really he was as handsome a fellow as any in Carolina.—Pompey then bowed to Mr.

Naylor, and said, "Mr. Naylor, if it be quite agreeable to your feelings, I will thank you to call me Captain; 'specially when you observe, sar, that my crew are present. I always wish to have good example before my crew." And here Pompey drew himself up with much state and gravity, with his arms folded across his chest. Mr. Naylor, who was in reality a very affable man at all times, smiled—indeed Pompey's speech excited a smile on the countenances of all present—and said, "Oh! very well; by all means Captain Pompey, I really made a mistake. Well, a prime negro, named Pompey, captain of the said schooner *Susannah*, 28 years old, sound, sober, and honest, well acquainted with the Georgetown and Savannah trade, and also with the turtle fishing on the Florida banks. Who bids for Captain Pompey? He will be a great acquisition to any one, especially to the owner of this same schooner. Is five hundred dollars bid?"

"Yes," said a would-be purchaser.

"Six hundred dollars, I hear—seven hundred dollars: thank you, Mr. Turner; eight hundred dollars— nine hundred dollars—one thousand dollars for Captain Pompey. Go on, gentlemen, you a'n't half-way yet. Captain Pompey is worth two thousand dollars, if he is worth a cent."

When the thousand dollars were bid I had my eye on Pompey, and being pretty well acquainted with him, felt much interested; and it was curious here to see the workings of human nature, or rather of human pride; at a thousand dollars Pompey held his chin at least three inches higher, and his jet black eyes actually flashed with excitement. However, to go on, eleven hundred dollars were bid—" Twelve hundred dollars, do I hear?" said Mr. Naylor; "thirteen hundred dollars—thirteen hundred dollars, is that all that is bid for Captain Pompey, the primest hand in all the coasting trade? It is actually throwing him away."

"Not so fast, Mr. Naylor, if you please," said Pompey, again interrupting; "whether you throw me away or not, you are 'ware, sar, that I shall not throw the *Susannah* away, nor myself either, if I can help it."

"Well done, Captain Pompey," said a bidder; "fifty dollars more for that, my lad."

Mr. Lawson, who had purchased the vessel, seemed considerably uneasy now. "At once," he said, "fifteen hundred dollars, Mr. Naylor; and that is my last bid."

"Fifteen hundred—fifteen hundred; does nobody say more? then fifteen—fifteen—fifteen hundred dollars;—going, going, gone! It is a high price, Mr. Lawson; but still you have a bargain, considering Captain Pompey's character and ability."

Mr. Naylor now proceeded,—" Jacob, a negro man, aged 30, sound, sober, and faithful, acts as mate; Cæsar, aged 25, of a similar character, acts as steward; and Jupiter, a negro boy, aged 16, a very promising lad, acts as cook : these three go in one lot. Terms for the whole of the negroes, cash on delivery."

Not to tire. the reader with the auctioneer's gossip, these three were knocked down to the gentleman who bought the other two lots, at two thousand dollars.

The sale being now finished, Captain Pompey
bowed low to Mr. Lawson and Mr. Naylor, and said,
" Gentlemen, I hope you will do me the honour, with
as many of the other gentlemen as choose, to step
down and take a glass of wine ; it will be most grateful to my feelings, and I beg you will not deny
me the felicity of entertaining you for once."

" Oh, yes, Captain Pompey, by all means," said
two or three at once; " we shall, with much pleasure, drink success to the *Susannah*, her captain and
crew."

The reader will have perceived that the whole of
the crew of the *Susannah* held office in one shape
or other, viz., captain, mate, steward, and cook.

Upon going below, the cabin scuttle being off,
I could hear Pompey order Cæsar to put down
glasses and bottles. He then drew some Madeira
wine, and had decanters of brandy and gin, on the
table besides. With his own hands, he then went
round with the liquor on a waiter, and served his
guests in a most respectful manner.

" Sit down a little, Captain Pompey," said the new
purchaser ; " sit down, and take a glass yourself."

" No, Mr. Lawson, I thank you very much, but
I know my station : I will not sit down in the presence of white gentlemen, and 'specially when one of
them is my owner; but I shall, with great pleasure,
drink prosperity to all consarned."

After a short time Pompey's guests left him, and
he then came on deck and requested me to go below,
where he acted the host with much suavity and

dignity. He sat at the head of the table, and placed me at his left hand, and we enjoyed ourselves eating, drinking, and perhaps too rashly criticising some of our white masters. Pompey did not forget his *crew* either; but called them down and treated them handsomely, *standing*, however. He knew his dignity too well to ask his subordinates to *sit*, especially when he had company.

The reader will, I dare say, see from all this that Pompey knew something of the world, and could act the courtier as well, perhaps, as many a one who sports a star on his breast, and an embroidered garter on his knee. Captain Pompey, it must be observed, however, although a slave, was treated by his owners in a very different manner from the common run of slaves. He was allowed a considerable number of perquisites, and many ways of turning a penny on his own account. In a few years after the time I refer to, he purchased his own freedom, and has since done well.

But in those days there were few obstructions by law to prevent a slave from procuring his freedom, provided he could satisfy his owner in regard to the dollars.

The case is totally different now. Since the attempted insurrection in 1822, various laws have been passed to prevent humane masters from emancipating their slaves, and enterprising and careful slaves from purchasing their freedom. In fact, such a thing cannot be done without express permission from the legislature of the state; and the different processes that must be gone through in order to obtain this, operate very nearly as a total prohibition to individual emancipation. It is somewhat akin to, but even more difficult to obtain, than procuring an act of Parliament in Britain for any important matter.

CHAPTER IX.

Zamba comments on American liberty—Inhuman treatment of domestic slaves by their masters and mistresses—Condition of the negroes in Carolina—Zamba hopes to revisit Africa—Saves the life of his white friend—Negro epistle — Zamba and Zillah meet again, in slavery—Zillah bought by Zamba's master.

I HAD now been nearly two years in America, *alias* Columbia, *alias* — by a horrible incongruity — the land of liberty! Liberty, forsooth! why, really Dame Liberty, with her long hair flying freely behind her, her bold look, and the cap of liberty in her hand, looks mightily out of place, as she appears in a gilded and splendid car, drawn by a score of groaning slaves, loaded at the ankles with half a hundredweight of iron shackles, and with their bare backs wealed and scarred with the cart-whip or the cowskin. But this is all of a piece with Jonathan's inconsistency: witness his flag—the so much boasted of national flag. What the stars signify I am not quite satisfied about; but to a certainty the stripes very fairly represent the slave's portion in the community. Jonathan ought to be ashamed to hoist it when sailing

upon the highway of nations—the free and open sea ;
—or when he comes within sight of any land where
true liberty dwells.

It will be imagined that I am in jest ; but I really
would, with all due deference for the people of America, suggest, by way of improvement to their flag,
that they should expunge the stars, and replace
them by their far-famed eagle; such as is represented
on their coins.   Though I would have the said eagle
drawn with a cowskin in its beak ; for the bunch of
arrows in one of its claws, I would substitute a bundle
of cigars ; and place in the other claw a grog-bottle.
These three symbols, in conjunction with the stripes
underneath, would far more truly and faithfully represent the propensities and tendencies of a nation of
despots and slaves—of tyrants and their victims—
than their present device.

And now that I am upon this particular point, let
me ask what the far-famed heroes and worthies of the
revolution ever effected for the cause of true and
rational freedom ?

In their celebrated declaration of Independence,
they state that all men are born free and equal ; and
that personal freedom is the rational and indis-
putable birthright of every man.

Now, unless it can be made out clearly by the
abettors of slavery, that coloured men are brutes,
destitute of mind and soul, they must plead guilty to
the glaring inconsistency of bursting asunder with
the one hand the chains and fetters of King George
the Third—which weighed so heavily upon their own

limbs—whilst with the other hand they were firmly and cruelly riveting chains and fetters, ten times more weighty and galling, around the limbs of their coloured fellow-men—their brethren : thousands and tens of thousands of them born and bred in the same land.

I saw lately, in a British newspaper, a paragraph stating that the late President Jackson had left no instructions in his last will that his slaves should be emancipated ; but that George Washington had done so. This is a gross mistake. I say it with all due respect to the memory of the great Washington—the father of his country—the brave, acute, and inde-fatigable general ; the disinterested hero who refused to accept gold or permanent honours as a reward for his labours ; the man who in private life bore a spot-less name : in short, the man who bore the character of a sincere follower of Christ. This—all this, and much more in his favour may be true : but alas !—foul spot on the escutcheon of the immortal Wash-ington ! he left his slaves—and a goodly number they were—he left them a legacy ! What was it ? The chains, the fetters, and the degradation of slavery ! It is of no use denying it. I may be scouted by many, even in free Britain, for daring to arraign, in any shape, the otherwise noble Washington ; but I merely answer in the words of the Latin proverb, " Magna est veritas, et prevalebit."—Truth is great, and will prevail. America's *military* heroes have never moved one finger in the cause of general and genuine free-dom ; anything that has been done in this way, has been by her *Christian* heroes, and especially by some members of the Society of Friends. More than one of these real friends of liberty and mankind have, at once, given freedom to their slaves by the score, and even in greater numbers.

But to return to my story:—I had been nearly two years in Charleston, and had witnessed little practical cruelty in regard to slaves. To be sure I had occasionally seen youngsters pretty severely chastised; but not without cause. Nothing very glaring came under my notice, until the following occurrence. One fine summer morning, about six o'clock, as I was preparing to go to the Store, I heard a dreadful screaming in the neighbouring yard, where a new tenant had come during the previous week. On looking out of my bed-room window, I saw a *white gentleman* with his coat off; he held a young negro woman by the arm with his left hand, whilst with the other he struck her, apparently with all his force, with a cowskin. The poor girl was naked to the middle; her back and bosom quite bare of course; the blood flowed at every stroke, and her screams were truly heart-rending: "Massa, dear massa! for God Almighty sake forgive me, and I'll never do so again. Do, dear massa! for mercy sake, be done!" Her cries and petitions were alike in vain, until at last the white brute—I cannot help calling him such, whether or not the reader may be displeased at this expression: whoever had been a spectator, as I was, I am sure would not think my words too strong,—worn out with exertion, let her go. On inquiry, I found that in cooking some coffee for him that morning the girl had mismanaged it in someway! And mark! reader—enlightened British freemen!—this man the world styled a *gentleman!* he was a lawyer, of considerable practice in the city. I can hardly describe how I felt on witnessing this outrage on humanity—this horrible insult to the modesty and tenderness of the weaker, (I need not say the *fair*) sex; this dreadful degradation of human nature. But after all, thinks I to myself, the degradation is chiefly on the part of the *gentleman.*

In the course of the day I related to Mr. Thomson what I had seen. "Oh! Zamba, that is nothing to what you might see.every day, were you upon some country estates. The people in town, for decency's sake, and perhaps, too, because they are more polished in their manners altogether, keep these things as quiet as possible. When they wish to chastise a slave, they send him to the workhouse, or sugar-house, as your black brethren call it; and there the poor wretch receives a regular lashing, according to law: that is to say, not more than thirty-nine strokes can be inflicted in one day; and for this accommodation the owner must pay half a dollar."

I brooded in silence over the matter; but the very next day, as fate would have it, I witnessed a still more melancholy scene. On passing through State-street, I heard screams and yells proceeding from a yard; and on peeping through a chink in one of the boards in the fence, I beheld a young girl, stripped to the middle, her hands tied to a post, used generally

M

for fastening ropes to for drying clothes upon; and behind her a young—*lady,* shall I call her? No, nor yet woman; but a she-fiend, in the semblance of a lady, deliberately striking her victim with a regular cowskin, making the blood start at every blow; and to make the punishment more severe, abusing the girl with her tongue, in terms very unfit for a lady to pronounce: "I shall teach you, you confounded black devil, to burn my best muslin gown; but take that— and that," redoubling her blows; "and if you ever do the like again, I shall have you flayed alive." The poor wretch, it seems, in ironing a gown of the lady's, had applied an iron in rather too hot a state; and now the meek-tempered mistress revenged herself at the expense of everything sacred and dear to the sex, by treating her worse than a dog.

I felt an impulse to leap over the fence and interfere in the matter; but a moment's reflection convinced me that I would merely make the matter worse; and should I dare to raise my hand against a white person, I already was aware that, *according to law,* I should forfeit my right hand.

I made some inquiries regarding the parties, and found that the lady was a Miss —— (I am strongly tempted to disclose her name), a young woman of twenty; very beautiful, according to white notions, accomplished and wealthy, and much admired by the other sex: in short, one of the toasts of the city.

On passing the house, a few days afterwards, I perceived her seated near an open window, performing upon the piano, and singing with really a melodious voice; and looking, for all the world, as people say, like an angel. But oh! alas, what a different part had I seen her perform a few days previously.

Ladies of free and glorious Britain, what would you have thought to have seen your fair sister of Carolina—the delicate, the refined, the intellectual, the admired and beloved of her family,—throwing aside the character of an angel in human shape, and assuming the office of a bloody and iron-hearted executioner?—Ye would weep, would ye not?—ay, and blush with indignation, to see your sex so horribly degraded. But, above all, would ye not congratulate yourselves that ye breathed a purer and holier atmosphere, and lived in a land where no such outrage against the majesty, and the dignity, and the modesty, of womankind could take place?

I commenced one day, about this time, in a contemplative fit, to enumerate the advantages and disadvantages which appertained to the lot of the negro in Carolina. In the first place, supposing that in Africa he was in the situation of a mere vassal or slave to his native prince— subject to all the caprices of his lord, and, in the matter of life and death, completely at his mercy— in being transported to America, in one sense, and perhaps, in more than one, his condition as a rational being was amended; he had the means of being instructed in the knowledge of the one only living and true God, and of living in a community, even though as a slave, far, far elevated above any-

M 2

thing he could ever have experienced in his native land. I candidly confess that I deem the first of these advantages sufficient to outweigh a whole host of disadvantages.

In the second place—previous to the laws which have of late years been passed, placing so many obstacles in the way of individual emancipation—by industry and frugality, the negro could, in many cases, obtain his personal freedom to a far more efficient extent, and in a state of society more consonant to the dignity of man, than he could ever have obtained in Africa.

But, on the other hand, imported as a slave from Africa, he was put up for sale to the first bidder, as if he were a four-legged brute; and were he to assume a partner of the other sex, to console his dreary condition, he could, at an hour's warning, be torn from wife and children, and disposed of to a new tyrant; and perhaps one yet more reckless than he had yet laboured under. In the next place, he was totally denied all means of intellectual culture; even the very elements of reading were forbidden fruit, by *law:* a fine of 100*l.* being the penalty levied upon any white man who should dare to teach a negro the alphabet. In the third place, the evidence of a coloured person is perfectly null and void in the case of a white person. I reckon these three the most prominent disadvantages under which the negro labours in America; but I might enumerate a thousand petty insults to which he may be daily subjected. To mention one, for instance: the most degraded ruffian, who wears a white skin, upon meeting a coloured person on the pavement, male or female, old or young, should the latter not instantly give way, that is, step into the kennel, ankle deep or knee deep, may, if he so incline (and it is often done), knock the poor negro down: this may serve as a sample.

The condition of slaves in the city is much preferable to the situation of those in the country; this will appear most plainly, from the fact, that nothing is more common in town than for a master, in the event of a slave behaving improperly, saying, " I shall sell you into the country, you rascal, the very next time you do so and so." This generally has a far more decisive and lasting effect than a chastisement with the cowskin. Slaves in the city, especially domestic servants, are in general well fed and well clad ; although it would appear very anomalous to an *English* gentleman to see a black footman standing behind his master's carriage, clad in glaring and handsome livery, but without shoe or stocking on his feet. This I have seen often enough, and the same carriage, by the bye, had painted on the pannels some splendid coat of arms. *Republicans* assuming the insignia of nobility ! It would almost cause a poor negro to laugh, though the cowskin were brandished in his face.

The condition of negroes in the country is often dreary enough, though not altogether either without its advantages. Upon many estates the negroes are set to task work. In this way, however, they have to work apart from each other, and consequently are more cheerless.   I am aware that in the West Indies negroes generally labour in *gangs* or companies, and beguile their labour with the song, and with mutual words of encouragement; but in Carolina I have seen forty or fifty in one large field, all apart, and all labouring in solemn silence.   By this plan of task work, however, a clever negro has his work over sometimes by three o'clock in the afternoon ; and he may then employ the remainder of the day, if near a river, in fishing, or in snaring small game, or in any way he chooses.

By *law*, a planter must allow each grown slave nine quarts of Indian corn per week, and one pint of salt; but nothing else: no not a salt herring even, or an ounce of meat to relish his corn.   Indian corn by itself will hardly make into bread, and is generally used by the negro in the shape of *mush* or *hominy* (a kind of pudding or porridge).   This allowance gives about two and a half pounds per day of grain ; and on some estates the negroes are allowed a small piece of garden-ground, and may keep a few fowls, or a pig.   By these means, in some cases they are tolerably comfortable in regard to food ; and as to clothing, there is either by law or custom a certain allowance of various articles per annum : but all depends upon the temper of the proprietor or overseer.

The condition, then, of the negroes varies just in proportion to the variety of disposition or caprice in their masters; which of course are about as various as their physiognomies.

To say that by *law* the negro is entitled to this or to that is all a mere mockery; for who is there to see these *laws* put in execution? or to whom is the aggrieved negro to make his complaint? Suppose that an avaricious overseer on an estate of two hundred negroes thinks proper to give them only six quarts of corn per week, how is this to be rectified? The affirmation of the white tyrant will be taken in evidence at any time; whilst the asseveration or oath of the two hundred negroes will not go for one pin's point. To talk, therefore, of any *law* in favour of negroes, while at the same time the solemn evidence of a thousand of these negroes is rejected with contempt, is merely adding mockery and insult to injury.

In regard to my own case, I had nothing to complain of; I was well fed, comfortably lodged, and had plenty of clothes; and received much kindness from my master, and all with whom I had immediate intercourse. I had no grieving thoughts or cares, except in regard to my poor wife and relations, in Africa.

After I had been about two years in Charleston, I asked Mr. Thomson whether or not he thought Mr. Naylor would allow me to embark in some slave-ship for Africa, and arrange matters so as to return with my wife to Charleston. I had felt so much of the benefits of civilization, and of the sublime hopes and ideas with which Christianity inspired me, that I had no wish to return to Africa as a permanent residence. I was now a close and attentive hearer of the Gospel;

and humbly hope that without any prospect of future personal freedom, I should on no account have fore-gone the advantages which I weekly, or oftener, derived from the preaching of the Gospel.

Mr. Thomson made my request known to Mr. Naylor, who in a few days told me that some friends of his, in Baltimore, were at that time building a ship expressly for the African trade; that she would probably be ready for sea in six months or so, and that he would make such arrangements as would ensure my safety from being over-reached by any captain; and also, that he would secure my return with my wife.

Such kindness and friendly interest in my behalf fairly overwhelmed me. I could only kiss Mr. Naylor's hand, and weep my gratitude.

It pleased Heaven, however, that I should never again behold Africa. But I must not anticipate my story.

About this time an occurrence took place which raised me very much in the estimation of all who knew me. I am quite aware that in relating such anecdotes I am exposing myself to the charge of egotism in a great degree: methinks I hear some one of my indulgent readers exclaim, "Why this sur-passes all I have ever seen in print; I can tell you, my good black fellow, that you are tolerably well provided with vanity." So be it, gentle sir, as long as I adhere to the truth I must be content to stand the smart of a few of the shafts of criticism, as many a better man has done before me, and will have to do as long as books are printed.

To proceed : my master one day ordered Mr. Thomson and myself to go down to a ship which had arrived from the West Indies, and make some arrangements in getting the cargo properly placed on the wharf where it was to be sold next morning. The ship lay across the end of one of the wharves, and was a few feet distant from the land ; in walking up the plank which reached to the ship's gangway, Mr. Thomson unfortunately slipped his foot, and was instantly swept by the tide, which runs pretty strong here, astern of the ship, and in a few minutes would have been far out in the harbour. At this season, sharks were tolerably plentiful about the harbour, ranging about for prey at all times ; so that poor Mr. Thomson, who could only swim a few strokes, was in imminent danger. I was quite used to the water in Africa and could swim like a sea-gull ; so without hesitation, kicking off my shoes, and throwing off my jacket and hat, which was done in a few seconds, I plunged into the flood, and after a few minutes' strenuous exertion made up to my friend, who was just at the moment sinking ; having seized him by the coat collar with my left hand, I continued to keep afloat until a boat (several of which were pulling hastily to our assistance) came alongside and hauled us in ; Mr. Thomson in a state of insensibility, and myself well ducked and completely out of breath. A tavern was luckily at hand, into which Mr. Thomson was conveyed, and by prompt attention was brought to his senses in less than an hour. As soon as he saw me and understood from those around that I had been his preserver, he held out his hand and said; "Zamba, I always thought well of you; but now I am bound to you for life: never shall I forget my noble-hearted Zamba." He was speedily conducted home to refresh himself in bed, and was out next morning at business.

This little incident, which I should have deemed a matter of no moment in Africa, procured me considerable favour and interest here. Mr. Naylor took me by the hand and was pleased to say: "You are a good boy, Zamba, and have behaved like a true hero, and a true Christian, which is more to the point; and depend upon it, you shall be no loser by your generous endeavour to save Mr. Thomson: you shall not want a friend as long as I am spared, and your conscience will be a satisfaction to you in life and death."

Mr. Thomson himself redoubled his attention to me, and made me spend at least every other evening in his room, instructing me as far as his own information went, and causing me occasionally to write him short letters, to which he gave answers. I am certain some of my attempts in this way would amuse the reader not a little. I have most of them yet in my possession, and frequently peruse Mr. Thomson's with a melancholy pleasure; he having now been nearly these forty years in a land (at least I believe and hope so, from the bottom of my soul) of light and glory, where no proud tyrant can presume to lord it over his trembling slave. Should these pages of mine be yet perused by some haughty Carolinian, no doubt he will say: " Ay, ay, the black scoundrel! and he pretends to sentiment too: could I but find out his den in Charleston, I should make a good cowskin welt his hide for him." Providence will, however, I trust, protect the poor old black fellow from the despots of Carolina: and who knows but these pages may live and bring forth fruit many years hence, and serve to stir up the next generation of negroes, at least to make an attempt to obtain their rights. I now give a literal copy of one of my first letters to Mr. Thomson. The spelling and diction will amuse the reader, no doubt; but could he only see the penmanship it would add to his mirth.

" VERRY GUD SAR,
I AM moch indett to yu for kindnes to poor Africann.—I'm stonish yu pay tension so grat to blak Slavv—if Scotsman al lik yu den Scotlan must shude bee vine cuntrey—yu teech me reed—reed Bibell.—Bibell telly me all bout God and Hevven an grat most eksselentest Saveeour Jesus who die for all men ever live and bleeve on Him.—Bibell telly me allsoe bout Hell, dat is de place vere al bad man goe—al Tyrands an Moorderurs an Teeves — dey wil floggee Cowskinn one anoder dere for punishe for sins dune in dis worlld—'Low me tank yu Massa Tomson fur al yur tension an no morr till nicks time yu heerre from mee yur moss bedeent Sarvan   ZAMBA."

For some months matters went on very smoothly with me; only that I was getting very impatient to know when the new ship spoken of would sail for Africa.   One day, however, in April 1803, Mr. Naylor came into the Store, and calling me aside informed me that a ship had just come into port consigned to him with a cargo of slaves direct from the river Congo; and he smilingly said, " Perhaps, Zamba, you may hear some news of your wife and friends." I felt very much agitated at this information; and felt something strange beating at my heart, I could not explain how.   Mr. Naylor a short time after- wards ordered Mr. Thomson and myself to proceed to the wharf where the ship had by this time hauled in, and make arrangements about the slaves coming ashore, &c.

I remained quite silent all the way, but felt as if something strange were about to happen.   When we came alongside the ship (the *Hunter*), the slaves were crowding out, and one-half were already washed and quartered in the sheds.

We proceeded thither to ascertain what kind of cargo we had got; I had just entered the little build- ing, and Mr. Thomson had stepped in the door-way, when I heard my name called, or rather screamed out, and, in a moment, a young woman had thrown her arms around me and continued calling out, " Zamba ! my dear Zamba."

In the first moment, although the voice somehow thrilled to my heart, I was, as the sailors say, " taken all aback;" but, on recovering myself, and looking

in the woman's face, my astonishment may be
imagined, when I found her to be my own dear
Zillah;—ay, the once proud and splendid African
princess. But, alas! how altered; not so much in
looks, however, as in apparel and general appearance. She had merely a short Osnaburgh petticoat
on her lower limbs, an old Madras handkerchief on
her head, and a tattered printed shawl across her
breast; but better, however, in respect to dress, than
the most of her fellow passengers. Alas! where was
now the rich and gaudy apparel in which I had her
clothed in her native land? where the many gold
ear-rings and bracelets, and the necklace of pearl,
which would have been coveted by many a European countess? These, however, were nothing
in my eyes, while here was my own beloved Zillah
herself, though considerably wasted and worn out,
yet to all appearance in good health. Need I say
that my delight far surpassed my amazement, and
this delight was heightened by the idea, which
instantly flashed across my mind, that as I was
in favour with my master, and had plenty of cash
in his hands, to procure my Zillah's freedom, all
would be right. Mr. Thomson remained silent for
some minutes; but as soon as my wife and I had
composed ourselves a little, came forward and con-
gratulated me on my happiness. "Why, Zamba,
this is quite a romance: it surpasses anything I
have ever seen in a theatre. I shall instantly talk
to Mr Naylor, and get him to make some arrangement with the captain regarding your wife; for if he

gets time to know your whole history, he will, no doubt, enhance her value to an exorbitant pitch."

Having arranged a few matters then, Mr. Thomson told me to remain and comfort poor Zillah, whilst he would inform Mr. Naylor regarding the affair, and he would also go home and send down one of the wenches (young negro females in Charleston are always styled *wenches*,—*girl* is the more genteel appellative of young white females) with a few clothes for Zillah. In about an hour Mr. Naylor made his appearance, and said, "Now, Zamba, it will be in my power to reward you for your fidelity as a servant hitherto, and for your humanity in saving Mr. Thomson, when in danger of being drowned, or devoured by sharks. I shall go on board, and can, I should think, easily make a bargain with the captain, for your wife." He then went on board, and in a few minutes sent for me; he wished, as he said, to make the bargain in my presence. After a short discussion, and having told the captain a little of my history, and said more in my favour than I deserved, a bargain was struck for three hundred and fifty dollars, hard cash. Need I say with what delight I witnessed and experienced all this. I was overwhelmed with gratitude to Mr. Naylor and Mr. Thomson, and, above all, with deep gratitude to the Great God, who had brought about, in such an unexpected way, my most sanguine wishes.

Mr. Naylor then told me to convey Zillah home, and he would make some arrangements with Mrs. Naylor to have her accommodated: "In fact," said he, after taking a good view of my wife, " I think, Zamba, that Mrs. Naylor will take her to wait upon herself. I am pleased with her appearance so far, and have no doubt she will soon learn to be a clever waiting-maid."

Zillah, before she left the shed, pointed out to me two or three women who had done all in their power on the voyage, to console and comfort her; and beseeched me to do something for them if I could. I was glad to find Zillah was still my own kind-hearted and grateful girl; and, at the sale, which took place in two days afterwards, by means of Mr. Thomson's influence, we managed to have these women, all of them, sold as domestic servants in the city: besides this, I made them a present of some useful clothing in the name of Zillah, who had the pleasure, years and years afterwards, of meeting frequently with her fellow-voyagers. In the fulness of my heart, I also gave a small handkerchief, or some trifle, to every woman who came in the *Hunter*, and a piece of tobacco to every male slave who could use it.

CHAPTER X.

Zamba and Zillah reunited—Tidings of home—Zillah's account of her
capture—Native missionaries needed for Africa—Zamba instructs
Zillah—Penalties for teaching a negro to read—Arrival of Zamba's
brother-in-law—Zamba and Zillah freed by their master—Zamba
a shopkeeper.

WHEN Zillah arrived, she could only speak a few
words of English ; Mrs. Naylor was pleased with
her, however, and under the government of such a
mistress, she soon became very serviceable in her
department, and could make herself understood in
English. She was allowed to take up her residence
in my little room, and I may say that I was now
as completely happy as man can be upon earth.
It may be imagined that after the first flurry of my
meeting with my wife was over, I should inquire for
my mother and the rest of my family. In a few
words, I learned, that my poor mother had died,
partly of a broken heart on my account, about six
months previously ; but that all of my sisters were
well, and my two brothers-in-law were carrying on
the government of my kingdom with much satisfaction to my subjects.

As to herself, Zillah informed me that after I had left her, she felt lonesome indeed, and day by day wandered hither and thither, especially by the banks of the river, often gazing to the westward, as if she would hear or see something of me. They did hear at last, by a round-about way, that I had been cheated by the captain, and left in Charleston : although totally ignorant of geography, yet Zillah could recollect the name Charleston well enough, and that Charleston was in America. Even after she had given up all hopes of ever seeing me, she still continued to keep a look-out upon the river ; and, being about a mile from her home one day, quite by herself, she observed a large boat rowing down the river, close to the side where she walked.

At last the boat put into a small cove a few hundred yards from her ; and some of the men, who were white, came ashore. She then observed two of them walk straight into the country ; but when they had proceeded about a quarter of a mile in that direction, they struck off at a right angle, and commenced running, as if chasing each other in diversion. They then took a turn about, as if to the river, and immediately made towards her. One came up on each side, and seizing her by the wrists, one of them drew a cutlass, and made signs, by pointing to her mouth, and then to her breast, that he would kill her if she screamed.

They then dragged her towards the boat, in which were about a dozen white men and a few blacks, put her in, and pushed off to the middle of the river;

N

and by hard rowing were not long in reaching their
ship, which lay at anchor in the river.

As soon as poor Zillah was in the boat, some of
the men attempted to take the bracelets and ear-
rings from her; but were instantly checked by a man
who seemed superior to the rest. She was no sooner
on board the ship than the same person took her
down to the cabin, where the Captain sat smoking;
and here poor Zillah was speedily stripped of all her
ornaments, pearl necklace included. She was then
without ceremony huddled down to the hold, and
for many days endured great hardships.

Whilst at sea she suffered much from sickness;
but when able to keep her feet was allowed to be on
deck for an hour or two every day. Here she could
make out, by the little English she understood, that
the ship was bound for Charleston. She felt quite
delighted at this, and her spirits rose thenceforth, as
she had some little hopes that she might meet with
me. The result was as I have already narrated; and
shows that although Providence may seem at the
time to be working quite in opposition to our dearest hopes and wishes, yet that oft in its mercy it
brings about, in a wonderful and mysterious way,
the very thing we had desired; thereby inculcating a
lesson of patience and submission under every seeming disappointment.

Having now obtained the dearest object of my
affections, I gave up all idea of ever visiting Africa:
although at times my conscience whispered me that
I, who had so largely partaken of the mercy of God,

and had my eyes opened to the light of the Gospel, should act in some effectual manner, so that my poor blinded brethren in Africa might also in some degree, through my means, have an opportunity of knowing the one true God. My conscience, I say, told me, that I ought to forego my own comfort and convenience, and that I should at all hazards return to Africa and impart to my fellow-men all that I knew about the Bible and a Saviour. These reflections often yet prey upon my mind; for I am fully convinced that the civilization and christianization of Africa, will yet be mainly effected through the means and exertions of Africa's own children, or their descendants.

The climate of the greater part of Africa is an insuperable bar to the exertions, however well meant— I mean, to the *effectual* and extensive exertions—of white men. How many enterprising and noble-hearted Europeans, especially Englishmen, have become victims to the climate of Africa! It is truly a melancholy circumstance to contemplate. Consider, for instance, the colony of Sierra Leone, which was established as a means of introducing civilization and Christianity into Africa. In the space of fifty years, it has, I understand, cost the Government of Britain between eight and nine millions of pounds sterling, and the lives of about twenty-five thousand white men, military and civil; and the actual benefit which has accrued to Africa is comparatively nothing.

Let Britain establish a few colleges or schools in some of the West India islands; let her then procure

N 2

natives of Africa, either from our colonies or from Africa itself, and give these natives a fair education, such as will befit them to civilize and Christianise Africa in their native tongue; let them, then, be despatched to Africa, not by ones or twos, but by scores, and let them have the means and knowledge for establishing trade with the various African chiefs; and I will venture to say that in this way more good will be effected in behalf of Africa, and a greater bar thrown in the way of the slave-trade by the expenditure of *one* million, than by all that the *nine* millions expended on Sierra Leone has yet done; and this without risking the life of *one* Englishman. I am too old now to attempt to do anything myself; but I hope my advice, although only that of a poor old African, may cause wiser heads to think on the matter.

Having now my wife to comfort me, I applied myself with more vigour than ever to my duties at the store; being determined to prove to my master that there is both honour and gratitude in a negro bosom. I applied myself also most closely to my education, and now felt it my duty to instruct Zillah. This was a task in which I had tenfold delight; and giving her instructions, as far as my own feeble light would admit of, in regard to the Bible and her Maker, was also a most agreeable employment. I also took her to church with me; and she very readily took up the English tongue, and seemed very eager to acquire a knowledge of religion.

About a year after Zillah's arrival an occurrence

took place in regard to my own acquirements, which I must not pass over. One afternoon, when there was nothing particular for me to put my hand to in the store, I had taken up a newspaper, and was reading my way through it as well as I could; keeping myself, however, rather in a quiet part of the store. I had placed the paper on the top of a large packing-box, and while spelling over it, a Colonel Morgan, who dealt with my master, and owned a plantation about twenty miles from town, happened to stray in; and in looking through the store for some goods of a particular description which he wanted, he came close upon me. I heard him instantly exclaim—and he was a gigantic, rough-looking fellow, with a voice like a speaking-trumpet —"Ha! what the devil is this? How do *you* come to read the papers, boy? How do you happen to read, I say?" I looked up very calmly and meekly, as I thought, and answered, " I was taught, sir."—" You were taught, were you, you black rascal! and who taught you, pray? If I knew the scoundrel I would break his bones."—" The person who first taught me to read," said I, " is out of your reach at present, Colonel; and, surely, I am doing no harm, sir."—" Do you bandy words with me, you infernal black dog?" said the gallant Colonel; " take that and be d—d!" he then let fly at me with a great heavy stick which he carried; but, luckily, I was in time, and dodging my head escaped his friendly salute. The stick, however, made a deep mark on the edge of the box, showing the good-will with which the blow was given; and proving, also, that hard and thick as African skulls generally are, had my head caught it, it would doubtless rather have discomposed me.

The noise which the noble Colonel made, attracted the attention of a number of people who were about the store at the time; and Mr. Naylor, who was writing at his desk, came forward, and inquired what was the matter. "Matter," answered the Colonel, "why are not you a fine fellow to be one of the authorities of the city, and teach your cursed negroes to read? Don't you know, as well as myself, sir, that you incur a penalty of one hundred pounds by instructing a black fellow to read?" —"Just speak a little slower, Colonel," said Mr. Naylor. "In the first place, sir, it was not I that taught that boy to read; he could read English, sir, however it may surprise you, before he left Africa; and farther, although there is a law forbidding negroes to be instructed, I am not aware that there is any law forbidding them to read anything that comes in their way after they *can* read? And let me tell you, Colonel, that had you injured that boy (who is my property, look you) with your stick, I should have made it cost you much more than the penalty you talk of. I take it very ill, sir, that you should lift your hand to any person, white or black, in my store; and I will just advise you as a friend, Colonel, to command your temper a little." An - old Scotch merchant, a very wealthy man, who dealt much about the store, here interposed his word.

" Dear me, Colonel, man; what 's the matter wi'
ye? Ye think, nae doubt, ye are amang yere neegurs at hame just now: ye may kick and strike
them as ye please, an' no ane to interfere wi' ye;
but I think ye shouldna meddle wi' your neighbour's
property, ye'll get yourself into a scrape may be."
" Ah! so you must poke in your word," said Mr.
Niven; " why it's all owing to you foreigners that
we have so much trouble with our infernal neegurs;
you are continually exciting them to rebel in one
way or other."—" Foreigners! gude feth, my braw
Colonel, if it were na for foreigners, such as I
am, ye wad craw less cruse; if we didna tak the
cotton an' rice aff your hands, ye wad hae naething
to eat but Indian corn an' alligawtors ; no, nor a
pair o' hale breeks to your hinderlands." A great
number of customers, both Jews and Gentiles,
had by this time gathered round the disputants;
but this speech of the old Scotsman, turned the
laugh so much against the gallant Colonel, that he
thought fit to retreat, growling vengeance against
d——d neegurs and foreigners.

The ship *Hunter*, in which Zillah had arrived,
was preparing to return to Congo, and it was understood that she would be a regular trader between
that river and Charleston. I got acquainted with
the steward, who was a countryman of my own, and
who had actually this last voyage been up at my
native town, and had seen and conversed with my
brothers-in-law; I, therefore, ventured to entrust him
(and he faithfully kept his trust) with a small trunk

containing a few presents to my friends. It was of no use to write a letter, as none of them would have been the wiser; but I sent a verbal message, informing them how Zillah and I were situated.

Well, the *Hunter* sailed away, and in the course of eight months what was my surprise one day when my brother-in-law Pouldamah entered the store. We instantly recognised each other; and as soon as I was satisfied that he had come as a free passenger, and had made a cautious arrangement with the Captain to take him back to Africa, my joy was great indeed. He told me that he could enjoy no rest or peace until he could ascertain my real situation. The Captain of the *Hunter*, whose name was Toomer, was not a bad fellow on the whole (although the reader will possibly recollect that he deliberately robbed poor Zillah of her jewels), and having done a good deal of business with him he made a bargain to go with him as passenger, and upon being landed safely again at his own village he became bound to pay the Captain thirty doubloons; and Bollah, my other brother-in-law, witnessed and guaranteed the bargain. Pouldamah then whispered me quietly that he brought a few barrels of bees'-wax, a few large pots of honey, and a few elephants' teeth with him; and says he, in my ear, " Zamba, I wish to have my small cargo ashore as quickly as possible, and secured snugly with you, as one of the honey-pots is much more valuable than the Captain or any of his men imagine." I instantly procured a dray, and went along with my friend, and speedily had all secured in Mr. Naylor's premises. On arriving at home, Pouldamah selected one of the honey-pots, and going up to my bed-room I found on examination that my considerate relation had placed a bag with a hundred doubloons, and another with ten pounds of gold dust at the bottom of the pot.

I appreciated his prudence, but could not help saying, "Why, my dear Pouldamah, had Captain Toomer but guessed the contents of this pot, decent fellow as he may be, considering his profession, I rather fear he would have played Captain Winton with you."

I can hardly express how delighted I felt at seeing Pouldamah, and although I was by no means in want of the money, I could not but feel very grateful. As I could not properly accommodate Pouldamah in my own small room, and did not wish to intrude too much on my master's condescension, I procured him comfortable lodgings in the house of a coloured friend; and here Pouldamah resided during five months: the ship requiring thorough repairs, and the Captain having fallen sick, caused this delay. Pouldamah could already speak some English; but during his stay in Charleston, I gave him a lesson almost every evening, and I engaged a clever mulatto friend, who devoted several hours every day to his instruction. Before he left Charleston he could read the Bible pretty correctly, though slowly, and could also manage to scrawl a few lines, so that I could understand him. I made up a handsome assortment of goods for him, and at length, with many tears, he parted with Zillah and myself.

When the *Hunter* returned, he sent me a letter as evidence that the Captain had dealt honourably with him, and I occasionally heard from him and of him for many years; but for these last fifteen years I have heard no intelligence whatever from Congo. I trust, however, that Pouldamah made good use of the knowledge he acquired in America, and that even now his posterity are deriving benefit from his enterprise.

Matters continued to go on smoothly with me and Zillah. We were as happy, I believe, as any couple in America. She brought me no more children, so we contented ourselves with one another as well as we could. I placed the gold Pouldamah brought me (and he assured me that he had a large quantity at home, but I told him I was quite satisfied, and would have him run no more risk in bringing or sending it to America) in Mr. Naylor's hands; and now it might be said I had a fortune. Mr. Naylor dealt with me like a true gentleman. I was allowed many perquisites about the store, and was in fact as much indulged as if I had been his own son.

In 1807, Mr. Naylor had regular free papers made out for Zillah and me ; but as long as he remained in Charleston he allowed us to remain with him. At length, when he gave up business and went to reside in another State of the Union, in 1819, he had a regular account-current made out for me from the commencement; allowing both Zillah and myself annual wages, and calculating interest upon the money he held for me to a fraction, and fairly and finally paid me over every cent of what was due.

My gratitude to Mr. Naylor and his family can only cease with life itself; and I can assure the reader, that in recording the virtues of white men, I derive ten times more satisfaction, than in dilating upon their failings and vices.

In 1819, I took a small shop, and continued for some years to carry on a limited trade; more for the sake of keeping myself in employment than for the sake of gain. For the last twenty years I have lived very quietly and retired, and spent much of my time in perusing the works of the " mighty dead." I also devote a little of my time and means in alleviating the distresses of others.

And now should the time and labour which I have expended, and mean yet to expend, in making the wrongs of my fellow-countrymen known to Europeans, and to those noble-hearted Republicans of America who really are free and consistent, and who are willing that the bonds of slavery should be broken—should my exertions, I say, come to any account, then shall I reckon these the happiest and the best spent moments of my life. I have anticipated my history here somewhat; but, as already mentioned, I have no regular plan laid down, and just write what comes uppermost.

CHAPTER XI.

Zamba and Zillah join a Methodist Church—Their reception by two
Ministers—Zamba and Zillah married—Zamba loses his White
Friend—Captain Winton in Distress—Is relieved by Zamba—
Winton killed in a Duel—A Carolinian Duellist.

I HAD now been a regular attendant at a Methodist
chapel for nearly four years, and for the last twelve
months had been accompanied by Zillah, as often
as her duties to her mistress would permit. She
had by this time made considerable progress in reading, and could get tolerably well through a chapter
in the Testament, and understood pretty well what
was spoken from the pulpit. It was now hinted to
me by some coloured members of the congregation,
that we should both of us wait upon the minister,
and apply to be admitted as church members; and,
further, that it would raise us in the estimation of
our brethren to have our marriage celebrated according to the Christian form.

It is well known to most people, that ministers
in the Methodist body are almost continually shifting
from one station or chapel to another. Our clergyman
at this time was a Mr. Gorman, a powerful preacher;

but by many thought rather bigoted and narrow-minded. However, we ventured to wait upon him, although I confess that I was under considerable trepidation regarding the way in which I guessed he would question me.

" Well, Zamba," said he, " one of the elders has spoken to me regarding you, and gives you a good character, and allows that you are a very regular church-goer; but you must not think that your good deeds, or anything that you can do, will advance you one step nearer to the kingdom of heaven; you must look upon yourself as a sinner damned to eternal perdition thousands of years before you were born. All men fell in Adam, and all of woman born are from their infancy prone to evil, and nothing else than children of the devil. How do you think, Zamba, that you can be saved from the wrath of God ? "

" I believe, Massa," said I, " that in Jesus Christ alone all men shall be saved. I read in the Bible that as in Adam all sinned, so in Christ shall all be made alive."

" You have said so far well, Zamba," answered he; " but the words of Scripture must oft be taken in a limited sense. You surely do not believe that *all* men will be saved ? "

" I cannot tell, Massa, exactly how that is; but does it not say that Christ is the propitiation for our sins, and not for our sins only, but for the whole world; and it is said that God will never require what he never gave. I should be grieved to think

that many of my countrymen who have lived peaceably, and done good to all around them, as I know
some have done, should be damned to all eternity,
when it was not in their power even to hear of
Christ."

"Zamba, Zamba," said he, "as long as you
think and believe in this way I cannot admit you as
a member of Christ's church : you are yet in the gall
of bitterness, and in the bonds of iniquity. You
must go home and pray that your eyes may be
opened to the truth."

"Hear me, Massa, if you please," said I. "Do
you condemn me for saying that I hope some of my
poor innocent countrymen may be saved? Does not
the Bible tell us to have charity for all men, and to
pray for all men ?"

"It does not matter, Zamba," said he; "I fear
some one has been putting erroneous notions in your
head. I tell you that, *all men—all men whatsoever,*
I say—are naturally and necessarily children of the
devil, and heirs of God's wrath ; and until they are
renewed in the image of Christ, and sprinkled with
his blood, they can have no hope—no title to hope
for salvation. I suppose it will be useless to ask
your wife any questions at present; so go home and
pray, and read your Bible, and come back in three
or four months, and we shall see then how your soul
fares."

I then left the clergyman rather disheartened and
downcast, I confess; and I could not, for my life,
see how charity for my poor blinded countrymen

could be a barrier in the way of my own salvation. Mr. Gorman was, however, removed to a station in the country about two months afterwards, and a new minister was appointed to our chapel.

After hearing him for three or four Sabbaths, I was so much pleased, and I hope edified, by his discourses, that I ventured again to risk an examination, and called upon Mr. Willison.

He received me in a much more sympathizing and kindly manner than his predecessor had done. The very tones of his voice thrilled encouragement to my heart; and after a few questions, nearly to the same purpose as those put by Mr. Gorman, and which I answered in the same candid manner, and nearly to the same effect, he said, " Zamba, I cannot blame you for wishing well towards your poor benighted brethren in your own land; but you see very plainly from the Bible, that there is none other name given under heaven whereby men shall be saved, but the name of the Lord Jesus Christ. I dare not, however, as a minister of the blessed Jesus, who himself, while upon earth, preached and practised love and charity to all men, without exception, put limits to his atonement. What he never gave, he never will require; and you will observe that Jesus himself said, that in the day of judgment it would be more tolerable for Sodom and Gomorrah, and, consequently, for such places as poor benighted, neglected Africa, than for such as had the benefit of the Gospel and rejected it. And you will also observe, Zamba, that when some of the disciples asked their

Master, whether *many* would be saved, he told them as much as to mind particularly their own salvation, and leave the rest with God, to whom all things are possible; and, finally, Zamba, shall not the Judge of all the earth do right? Strive ye, Zamba and Zillah, and pray without ceasing, that your own souls may be enlightened in the first place, and pray frequently for all men upon earth. Do your duty to all and to each other as far as in you lies, and believe in the Lord Jesus Christ, and thou shalt be saved."

Having put a few questions to Zillah, which she answered in a natural and simple manner, considering her opportunities as yet, he said it would be cruel in him any longer to debar us from coming to the table of the Lord! Shortly after this, in the presence of a few friends, we were regularly joined in wedlock, and at the same time admitted to partake of that bread which is unto Everlasting Life, and of which whosoever eateth shall never die. I now felt pleased and gratified (I hope without pride) that poor Zillah and I were members of a Christian community, and members of Christ's body.

Nothing remarkable occurred with me for a considerable time. In the year 1807, the yellow fever raged to a great degree, and to my inexpressible grief I lost my excellent friend Mr. Thomson. The yellow fever is a great scourge to the Southern States of America. It is supposed by some to arise from the putrid exhalations of decayed vegetable matter in the low, swampy, country; and by others it is sup-

posed to be imported from other parts,—such as the
West India Islands, especially Cuba, and South America.—It is very fatal, at all events, in its effects,
amongst the white inhabitants, especially strangers.
Upon an average, I believe that seventy or seventy-
five die out of every hundred who are affected by it,
and it gives very little time of preparation for death.
Mr. Thomson was attending his duty in the store in
the morning; but after breakfast complained of a
pain in the forehead and in his back. In an hour or
two he was obliged to betake himself to bed. Mr.
Naylor requested me to wait upon him, and medical
aid was instantly procured; but the fearful malady
made such rapid progress, that he died the third
morning, and was consigned to parent earth in the
afternoon of the same day.—Corruption makes such
rapid progress in this climate, and especially in cases
of yellow fever, that there is a necessity for almost
immediate interment. Poor Mr. Thomson was sensi-
ble nearly until the last struggle, and about two hours
previously, when the black vomit had attacked him,
he knew that all was over.

"Zamba," said he; "poor Zamba, I am sorry to
leave you. But all men are born to die; and if my soul
is found in Christ, which I humbly hope is the case,
it is perhaps much better to go away in my youth,
than to remain to combat with a cruel world, and
after all, perhaps, go astray, and depart from the
Saviour. I am convinced that finally everything that
happens upon earth must be for the good of man. But
I feel faint, Zamba, and can only say that I wish you

o

well. Go on as you have done, and I hope we shall
hereafter meet in a land of light and glory—of love
and peace, where no sorrow enters, and where God
shall wipe away all tears—where there are no tyrants
and no slaves—where Europe's pale sons and the sable
sons of Africa, are alike welcome—where, in short, all
is light, and where darkness and sin are for ever unknown."

He spoke only a few broken sentences after this,
and when he drew his last sigh, I felt for the time as
if I were alone in the world.   Peace to thy soul, my
noble-hearted friend ! Though nearly two score years
have rolled over my head since I saw thy mild eyes
close in death, often and often does old Zamba, heave
a sigh for the warm-hearted and youthful Scotsman.

I now felt the absence of Mr. Thomson as a deep
and irreparable loss : but being engaged busily in the
store from morning till night, and having my faithful
Zillah to console me, time, that soother of grief, by
degrees reconciled me to my loss.

In the following year, an incident occurred which
showed that sooner or later, Providence will not suffer
the wicked to go unpunished, and verifying also the
proverbs, " Easy got, soon gone," and " What comes
by the wind, goes by the water."

One afternoon who should I see enter the store and
inquire for Mr. Naylor, but my old acquaintance,
Captain Winton : but in appearance and habiliments,
alas ! how fallen.   He plainly perceived me, but
went to the back part of the store where Mr. Naylor
was at his desk, and I could perceive that he re-

ceived a parcel of money from him. He repeated his visits several times, but I could perceive that although Mr. Naylor always gave him more or less, it was in the way of charity. Mr. Naylor, by-the-by, was a very benevolent man; I have seen him give a person in distress again and again a twenty dollar note, and more than once, fifty dollars. The captain seemed now terribly chop-fallen; he had a most debauched look, and was generally half-seas over. He still kept up a swaggering appearance, however. I soon learned, on inquiry, that he had entered into some speculations in the north, which had turned out very unsuccessful, and that finally he had fallen in with gamblers and sharpers, and, to use an American expression, had got *close-shaved*. He had now come to try his luck upon a venture, at the cards and dice, in the south. I may inform the reader that I really felt sorry for him: but I rather fear that there was so much of the old Adam in my heart, as created a certain degree of satisfaction, or —(I am rather at a loss to find a proper word to express my feelings,) a sort of calmness or composedness in my breast when I reflected on the ways of Providence. About a month after his first appearance, one afternoon while I was engaged at some business on the wharf next to our store, Winton came up to me and said, " Well, Zamba, how do you get on? I hear that you are getting rich. I hope you haven't forgot old friends. Why man, Zamba, I am mighty particularly hard up for a ten dollar bill to-night, suppose you advance me so much; I shall repay you first chance I have." I looked very calmly at him and said, "Why, Captain Winton, I am sorry you have managed so badly with the money you had of me. I do not wish to insult a man in distress, but of all persons in the world, I never thought you would have applied to me for money." "Oh! well, well, Zamba, it is an old story now. But the fact is, I was under a strong temptation, and you must allow that in my situation, some persons would have treated you worse—ay, left you without a rag to your back, or a cent in your pocket: and, besides, you must admit that I procured you a good berth, and a good master." "Well," said I, "Captain, as things have turned out, I owe you no grudge; and to convince you that I am profiting by my instructions in Christianity, which enjoins me to return good for evil, if you meet me here to-morrow afternoon, I shall bring you what you are in want of; and in the mean time here is all the change I have upon me." I handed him a dollar and a half, and he actually dropped a tear on my hand as he shook it, and said "Zamba, you're a noble fellow. If certain white men I have lately dealt with, had such hearts as you, I should not be in this condition to-night." The next day I met him and handed him a doubloon, which quite astonished him; and in about two weeks afterwards I gave him another, but recommended him to try and get some employment.

After this I saw him no more until the following circumstances occurred a few weeks afterwards. Mr. Naylor had a summer-house in Sullivan's Island, to which he frequently resorted to enjoy the sea-breeze, and freer exercise than the city afforded; and I generally accompanied him to carry his gun or umbrella. One morning he went out about six o'clock, and I followed him of course. He took the direction to the north-east part of the island, where there was a small natural plantation of myrtles and other trees, and as we approached this spot, we observed thirty or forty men crowded together, and in a few seconds heard the report of two fire-arms. We were only an instant in being up with the group, and lo! here lay poor Captain Winton on the ground in the pangs of death. My master and I tried to hold up his head a little; and he turned his eyes upon us, and seemed to know us, but gave only a shiver or two and all was over. He was shot clean through the body. His antagonist was standing by, very coolly wiping his pistol, and most of the others seemed to look upon the matter as nothing extraordinary. Mr. Naylor was one of the magistrates of the city, and the fellow who shot Winton, being informed of this by one of the by-standers, instantly hurried off with a companion or two.

To show the systematic way in which duels are sometimes conducted in Carolina, I may mention that poor Winton's second stooped down, and examining the wound, remarked, as calmly as if he had been looking at a scratched finger, " A d—d good shot, by G—!"

I assisted with some others in carrying the lifeless clay to the hotel in which Winton had lodged whilst living; and in the afternoon he was interred in the burying-ground on the island, attended by a few heartless strangers. On inquiry, I found that a dispute about some game at cards the previous evening was the origin of the quarrel; and of thus causing one hardened sinner to hurry another, without a minute's preparation, into the presence of a God who has said, "Thou shalt do no murder." At one period this circumstance would have afforded me, I am sorry to say, a secret satisfaction; but now I was inclined more to sorrow than anger.

CHAPTER XII.

Description of Charleston—Negro Incendiaries—Traits of Slavery—
Gardens and surrounding Country—Extraordinary escape—The
Wilds of Carolina—An Inn in the Woods—Sporting in the Forest
—A Negro Patriarch.

I HAVE brought my personal narrative nearly to a
conclusion; but I crave to be indulged in making
a few observations, and relating a few anecdotes
regarding the moral and physical condition of Carolina. I am aware that the southern States of America
have not been so minutely described by travellers as
the northern, and therefore the more readily assume
the task.

The city of Charleston was founded about the year
1666, and is situated upon a peninsula, or neck of
land, bounded on the south by the river Ashley, and
by the Cooper on the north. These two rivers, which
are less than a hundred miles in length, and only
rank as sixth or seventh rate rivers in America, unite
at the city, and form an estuary or frith, which leads
easterly to the Atlantic, about ten miles distant.
The north side of this estuary, where it joins the

ocean, is bounded by Sullivan's Island; and the south side by John's Island and part of the mainland. There is a sand-bank or bar across the mouth, caused by the rolling of the Atlantic and the sand brought down by the rivers. This bar shifts frequently, and is at times very dangerous to vessels. It has been said, however, that it serves as a protection to the city from hurricanes, which generally come in this direction; and it is most assuredly a safeguard against any foreign enemy, as no vessel larger than a 36-gun frigate can cross the bar, and even then with difficulty, at spring-tides. On this part of the American coast, the tide rises and falls only about six feet.

There is a fort on Sullivan's Island, and one on the opposite island, also another nearer the city; but some of these are now dismantled of their cannon. There are some very heavy guns in Fort Moultrie on Sullivan's Island; and, during the revolutionary war, the British, who had intruded so far with a few frigates, actually came off second best in the affair. They succeeded, however, two years thereafter, in storming and taking the city, which was almost burned to the ground: but whether by the British or the Americans themselves does not appear clearly. The Americans at this time, to confess the truth, were very harshly treated by the British; and had they only evinced one-tenth part of that sympathy for the welfare and interests of their black brethren, which just and consistent men, struggling for their own freedom and rights would have done, I should consider them as martyrs and heroes in the cause of liberty. But when they only fought and bled for *a part* of the population of America, leaving the others in hopeless chains, I can only say, alas! for poor human nature. Many hundred of Carolinian patriots were at this time confined in close and crowded prison-ships, lying in Charleston harbour during the sickly season, and perished in a most pitiable manner in sight of their own fire-sides. There are some few aged people yet surviving in Charleston, who remember these things, and who shrink with abhorrence at the name of a British soldier—and no wonder.

Charleston is built partly of brick, but mostly of wood. Some of the brick houses are three or four stories high, and very handsome and substantial; though the huge wooden houses, with the elegant piazzas and balconies all gaily painted, are much more showy. The streets run mostly at right angles, and some of them are very broad and airy. There is generally a foot-pavement at each side, made chiefly of brick; the middle part for carriages is nothing but the bare soil or sand, excepting a few of the principal business-streets, which are paved in the middle with whinstone from New York or Scotland: this was done at great expense. Many of the streets are planted with fine shady trees along the edge of the pavement, looking very pleasant, and affording protection from the powerful rays of the sun. Several of the principal churches and other public buildings were erected during the British sway, and are some of them handsome and solid edifices.   Upon the whole, Charleston is one of the handsomest cities in the Soutnern States.

Charleston has unfortunately, like all cities built chiefly of wood, suffered greatly from fire.   More than once since I resided in it, at least one-half of the city has been completely destroyed within twenty-four hours; and I am quite aware that most of these fires have originated from the prevalence of slavery.   Revenge is one of the strongest passions which can affect the human mind; especially the mind of a man who has received no education, and who is daily subjected to degradation, insult, and tyranny.   Numbers of poor infatuated blacks have suffered on the scaffold in Charleston for incendiarism; and in many instances the poor wretches have confessed with their dying breath that they had no particular object in raising a fire, but merely to cause a stir, and in some cases to be revenged on massa for some trifling matter.   I have said, and will yet make it more clear, that the white lords of the creation do not enjoy their privilege of trampling upon the African race, either with honour or ease. During a whole winter, I have known the alarm of fire to be given almost every night, and sometimes four or five times in a night, and always more or less damage done.   Let the reader reflect what a melancholy state of things must exist in a city, where not only firemen and fire-engines must be called into service almost nightly, but where again and again loaded cannon with their attendant artillerymen, have to be planted at the corners of streets, ready to vomit death and destruction on that portion of the community who are by law and custom so cruelly oppressed, that no faith or trust can be placed in them. Were the poor blacks but allowed their rights as men and reasonable beings, they would be the very first to use their utmost endeavours to quench any accidental conflagration ; but, as matters now stand, the majority of negroes seem actually to enjoy an extensive fire, delighted that they can give their white masters so much trouble and vexation.

Charleston has also suffered much from hurricanes. I recollect one in September 1822, which was truly awful ; it left the city next morning in as ruinous and roofless a state as if it had undergone a regular bombardment, and many valuable lives were lost. To give the British reader an idea of the force of the wind, I can assure him that I have seen large trees broken off about four feet from the ground, as cleanly and evenly as if cut asunder by a saw. The very brick pavements were in some places torn up, and a hole left large enough to hold a wagon. Much damage, as a matter of course, was done to the shipping, and several vessels were seen outside the bar bottom upwards.

Some of the churches in Charleston are very handsomely fitted up inside, and to the credit of all denominations be it said, one side of the gallery is in all cases appropriated to the use of white strangers, and the other half to negroes.

In Charleston there has been always a handsome and commodious theatre, and during the winter

season this house of vanity is much better filled
and frequented than any of the churches ever are.
I never had the honour, however, of being within the
door of a theatre, so I can give no description of
what is inside ; for, by *law*, no negro or coloured
person can be admitted to the theatre in Charleston :
there is generally at the foot of the play-bills—
" *N. B.*, No coloured persons or dogs can be admitted." Mr. Thomson informed me that he believed negroes were debarred from entering such
places for this reason, that in some of the plays acted
black men or women held too conspicuous and too
exalted a position. Does not this display something
akin to fear on the part of the whites ?

Charleston contains about 40,000 inhabitants,
whereof only three-eighths are whites ; the remainder are blacks and coloured persons, of whom
about 3000 are *free :* but their freedom amounts, in
reality, to little more than mere exemption from personal violence. They cannot, it is true, be sold on a
table like a piece of linen or cotton, but they
hardly possess one privilege over the merest slave,
although some of them are very wealthy. I knew
one very intelligent coloured man who petitioned the
legislature for leave to keep his carriage : but no, it
would not do. He was permitted, however, to keep
a drosky, or something of that sort, but not a four-
wheeled coach.

With regard to mulattoes, I have seen individuals
sold at Vendue who were two or three shades whiter
than mulattoes—whiter, indeed, than many native

Carolinians; but who had, as it was expressed by their proprietors, " *a drop of the devil's blood in them.*" I saw a little boy and girl of nine or ten years of age, sold one day, who were exceeding fair and beautiful; they might, indeed, have travelled through old England without suspicion of being allied to Satan by blood. They were purchased by *their own mother;* and in this one case I was much gratified to observe that intending purchasers who were present, on being apprised of the state of the matter, kept rather aloof, and offered no opposition to the poor mother, who, consequently, *obtained her own children* at a *very moderate* price.

In Charleston, all white men above eighteen and under forty-five years of age (with certain exceptions) are required to turn out as militia men.   There are a few uniform companies, gaudy and showy enough in appearance, but who would cut a sorry figure before a regular British regiment.   The majority turn out in their every-day clothing, and present rather a motley group; they serve, however, to keep a rabble of poor unarmed negroes in awe.   At a review of the Charleston *forces* I have seen a whole company or two stand out of line, and describe a complete semicircle, in order to avoid standing in a part of the field which was somewhat wettish.   Notwithstanding all that their officers could say or do, none of them would budge an inch.

Charleston covers a large extent of ground in proportion to its population.   There are many fine gardens in the rear of the houses, adorned with

orange, fig, peach, and other trees, and flowers of
various scent and hue, which I am not botanist
enough to describe. One splendid shrub, called the
magnolia, flourishes in great perfection; and I have
seen a species of small rose, called the multiflora,
spreading over a fence to the extent of perhaps thirty
feet by six or eight, and in all that space you could
hardly have put down your finger without touching a
rose. Kitchen vegetables are very difficult to rear in
or about Charleston, and consequently the price is
high, though a supply of cabbages, onions, &c. is
received by almost every vessel coming in from the
northern states. Nearly thirty years ago I saw a
single cabbage (but it was very large) sell for
eighteenpence sterling; and a quarter dollar was
common enough for one. The public markets in
the city are very commodious, and cleanly kept.
These consist of a range of sheds, supported on pil-
lars, and provided with tables, hooks, &c. at each
side, running up the whole length of Market Street.
There is a carriage-way betwixt these sheds and the
houses at each side, so that a busy scene is oft presented in this street. Large flocks of turkey buz-
zards, and a species of vulture of a most hideous
appearance, parade up and down this street throughout the day, picking up all kinds of offal. They may
be styled the city scavengers, and are protected by
law; a fine of 5*l.* being imposed on any person who
kills one of them. These birds regularly leave the
city every evening before sunset, and cross the Ashley
River to the woods, where they roost, and come

back in the morning as regularly as an organized body of men could do. It is curious to see the poor things on a cold day huddled in crowds around the chimney-tops for the sake of a little warmth.

The environs of Charleston present few agreeable walks; at least not such as I have seen by the river side in my native land, or as I have heard are to be enjoyed in great perfection in Britain : there is no such thing as a walk on the flower-enamelled velvet lawn. To attempt a walk by the banks of either the Ashley or Cooper rivers, you would find yourself up to the middle amongst reeds and mud.

Charleston lies upon a perfect level, and the country for 100 or 120 miles from the coast does not rise 20 feet above tide water. In all that region, not a rock, nor a stone so large as a man's head is to be found. Beyond this, the land rises apace, and at 200 miles distance from the Atlantic the ground is about 800 feet above sea-level. It here presents a beautiful variety of hill and valley, and sparkling mountain-stream, and is deemed quite healthy. Farther back, the land becomes still more elevated, and is in many districts peopled with not a few bears, wolves, panthers, &c. : but the inhabitants do not suffer great annoyance from the ferocity of these denizens of the forest, which must in general be sought after before they are met with. There are, however, even in the most cultivated parts of the low country, serpents of a dangerous and troublesome description, and in the rivers there are a considerable number of alligators.

I shall here relate a circumstance which I witnessed, although aware that some of my readers will think I am dealing in the marvellous : but I am only relating the truth. Mr. Naylor and his wife, accompanied by a young lady of about twenty, and a gentleman, left the city in their carriage upon a visit to an estate in the upper country near Columbia, and took me with them. When we had proceeded about sixty miles, which was not till the second day of our journey, we halted about noon by the road-side, to take some refreshment, as is usual in this country even with people of the greatest wealth. The carriage was drawn up near the edge of a clear stream which crossed the road with a gentle ripple; for there was a trifling descent in the ground at this spot. Mr. Naylor and his wife were walking about; the young gentleman was washing his face in the brook, and the young lady had seated herself underneath a steep bank. While the coachman was busy with his horses, and I was employed in spreading a cloth on the ground and setting out the refreshments; the young lady called out in a faint voice, " Look here ! but for God's sake do not stir or speak—one of you." Being all of us within thirty yards of her, we perceived to our horror and dismay that an immense black snake at least eight feet in length, and as thick as a man's arm, had fairly twisted itself round the poor girl's waist, and again bringing its head under her arm, was actually moving its head from side to side, and gazing in her face. The young lady remained perfectly still, but was

pale as a corpse, while the snake continued for about
two minutes to play or amuse itself in this manner.
The lady still kept her eye upon it; and at length,
to our infinite surprise and relief, it gently unwound
itself and glided away amongst the bushes. Some
of us were for pursuing it; but the young lady
begged of us to let it alone, as she had received no
harm. We were all much astonished at the circumstance, and were at a loss whether most to admire
the gentleness of the reptile, or the courage and
presence of mind of the lady. The snake was not of
a poisonous nature, but being of the constrictor
species, was of such a size that, had it been so
disposed, it could in spite of our interference, have
crushed the poor girl in a fearful manner.

In this excursion, the scenery was rather of a monotonous character: after leaving the city there was
little variety. Immensely tall and slender pine-trees
lined each side of the road, which consisted of the
bare sand, into which the carriage-wheels sometimes
sank from six to twelve inches, which made the pace
very heavy and slow. In general, we appeared to be
travelling through an interminable and gloomy lane,
and but for the occasional tinkling of the bells of the
wagoners' whom we met, and the chirping of birds by
the wayside, the dullness would have been intolerable:
at least to towns' people, who delight in a bustle.
Here and there we came to a cleared spot; but these
clearances, in proportion to the land in a state of
nature, were " few and far between," as some Eng-

P

lish poet says the visits of angels are to this poor fallen world of ours.

The first night we put up at a tavern about forty miles from Charleston, kept by a widow, who owned some land, and about twenty or thirty negroes, and seemed a very pleasant woman. There were a few strangers in the house, else I should have imagined we were altogether out of the world, the situation of the house was so sequestered. About ten acres immediately around it were cleared ; but the prospect in every direction was bounded by trees of a hundred and fifty feet high, forming, as it were, a sombre wall, enclosing us on every side. I measured some pine-trees lying on the ground, and found them to be one hundred and seventy feet in length, but not more than two feet in diameter at the thickest end. About sunset, it was curious to observe the various kinds of domestic animals arrive from their feeding place. First came a few cows with a bull at their head, at whose neck hung an old bell ; next a flock of sheep led by a ram, who had two plates of old iron jingling at his neck ; a flock of goats followed ; then a herd of swine ; and lastly, a whole squad of turkeys, geese, cocks and hens. The commotion and confusion of sounds that the poor creatures kept up, until admitted to their respective pens, was quite a contrast to the previous silence, and recalled to my mind the words of Scripture, " The ox knoweth his owner, and the ass his master's crib."

This being the first night I had slept in the country since I had been in America, everything seemed strange, and I could obtain little rest, but lay listening to the noise of crickets and insects of various kinds, the croaking of millions of bull-frogs, the hooting of owls and other night birds, and the incessant, yet pleasing, note of the Whip-poor-Will.

Two or three parties of wagoners encamped for the night about two hundred yards from the house, and I amused myself with watching their proceedings. They loosed their horses in a twinkling, fastened them to the wagons, and provided them with corn and water. In a few minutes afterwards a large quantity of wood was cut down, and in less than no time, as one might say, they had a fire blazing large enough to roast an ox; a large kettle was boiling for coffee, and a frying-pan with a handle five feet long, was hissing and frizzling with good solid bacon. One of the waggoners came into the tavern after supper, and got a large bottle filled with whisky, and soon afterwards I noticed that they all lay down on the ground in their great-coats, with their feet towards the fire, having two or three large dogs for sentinels.

At this period, there was an immense traffic upon this road betwixt Charleston and the upper country ; and many thousands of bales of cotton, and other produce, were brought down to the city in wagons. I have seen two hundred wagons in one morning arrive in King-street ; but of late years, since steamboats and railways have come into operation, there is hardly a wagon to be seen, and the country roads are consequently almost as lonely as an African desert.

About a hundred yards in rear of the inn here, there was a row or street of rude wooden huts for the negroes to reside in. I went into several, and found from the conversation of the inmates that they were tolerably comfortable, and by no means hard worked. There are not, however, many proprietors in Carolina so humane and indulgent as Mrs. Kinnon was.

I found here an elderly negro man busily employed in erecting a little frame-house, much superior to the others. His mistress had supplied him with boards and a few other necessary articles; and he had managed, with a little assistance from a fellow-servant and his own children, to cut down trees of a fitting size, and with his axe and saw and a few old chisels, had squared and formed all that he wanted in the way of joists, rafters, lintels, &c. The building was about twenty feet by twelve, and about eight high, with a regular sloping roof. He was putting shingles on the roof the night I saw him. These are flat slips of board about eighteen inches long, by five or six inches in breadth, and serve the same purpose as slates or tiles in more civilized countries. Poor old Jem had no nails to fasten them on with, and was doing it in his best way with wooden pins; indeed he had put the frame of the house together, and even boarded it, all with wooden pins. He had left openings for windows and a door, but said that he would be rather at a loss for hinges and some other articles of iron.

He seemed very proud of his new building, and I had the satisfaction of making him perfectly happy, as he said, by promising to send him a box next week, with a few pounds of nails, some hinges, a lock or two, and (what to him seemed better than all) two or three dozen small panes of glass. These articles only cost me about four dollars in all, and I sent them out, as promised, by a wagoner who passed that way, in about ten days thereafter. So assiduous was old Jem in his work, that when I saw him he was labouring by the light of a small fire; which some of his children kept burning brightly a few yards off, by means of chips, branches of trees, but especially by immense fir-cones which they procured in the surrounding forest. Some of these cones were as large as a seven-pound sugar-loaf, and being full of resin or pitch, burned with a clear and strong light. Jem was an African as well as myself, but from another part of the coast. He acknowledged to me that, slave as he was, he preferred the life he now led to what he could recollect of Africa ; for, said he, " I am now good Christian, and go every day to meeting, which is three miles off ; and although there is much *cowskinning* on some of the neighbouring estates, there is none of the continual murdering and fighting and burning as used to go on with my tribe and their neighbours in Angola. If I could only read Bible I should be so happy."

The next morning I was up with the dawn, but so tall were the trees all round this little farm, that we did not see the jolly face of the glorious sun until he was more than an hour above the horizon. About seven o'clock, a white man, carrying an immense turkey-cock over his shoulders, came in from the woods. " Mrs. Kinnon," said he, laying down his game in the piazza, " I must have an extra glass of bitters this morning. I have brought you a forty-pounder, I calculate; but I have had a long dull night of it waiting for this big fellow." The size and beauty of this bird was astonishing. I took it up by both legs, and when I held it up in front higher than my face its head lay on the ground. Its plumage was really splendid; its legs were about as thick as the wrist of a boy of twelve years old; and its spurs were at least four inches long. We guessed its weight to be over 40 lb.; and the man who shot it, assured me that he had killed turkeys in Carolina which weighed close upon 60 lb.; he had shot the hen only a few days previously. The way he did was this: he went to the haunt of the birds the evening before, and kept up a calling or gobbling noise similar to what is made by these birds, so as to keep his prey near to him all night; and as soon as daylight enabled him to spy the bird perched upon a tree, he took aim with his rifle, and brought it down with a single ball. He informed me that deer were tolerably plentiful, and that there was occasionally a sprinkling of wolves. Then pointing out to me two tremendous dogs, which were terribly marked and cut about the head; "These," said he, " are powerful critters, but a wolf, such as I never saw before, engaged with both of them about three weeks ago, and had I not interfered with my rifle, I rather guess that my two good dogs would have been regularly done up. The critter was a strapper, I tell you; he measured nearly seven feet including the tail."

As my master did not order his carriage till ten o'clock, I had time this morning to look about me a little. Seeing an old black man in a corn-field close by the house—and hearing him, too, for he made the forest re-echo with a shrill scream every half minute or so—I asked who he was. The people told me it was old Monday, and that he was 104 years old. On going up to him, I could see that he was indeed a patriarch: his hair was white as snow, and not a tooth was left in his head; he held a long staff in his hand, and kept up an incessant noise and screaming to frighten the birds, as I understood; he had an old pair of Osnaburgh trousers on, and an old blue jacket, but neither shirt nor anything else. He appeared to be in his dotage, and I could make out little of what he said; but I found that he had come from Guinea when about twenty years old. I offered him a small piece of silver money; he looked at it and then returned it to me, shaking his head; but he took a stump of a tobacco-pipe from his pocket and pointed to the bowl of it, which was empty. There was no mistaking this language, so I pulled out a good junk of tobacco and gave it to him. He then seemed to meditate a little. There were no lucifer-matches in America in those days, but I had a powerful burning-glass in my pocket, and as the sun is always strong in Carolina, I had his pipe blazing for him in no time. He seemed quite petrified at what I had done, and eyed me rather suspiciously at first, but presently puffed away most vigorously. Poor old Monday! thinks I; what a tedious and dreary pilgrimage you must have had. Surely the grave will be indeed a bed of rest for you, and the God of mercy and of love will never require such an account from you, as from those who have all their days lived in ease, and had every opportunity of moral and intellectual culture!

CHAPTER XIII.

Scenery of South Carolina—Cotton and Rice Plantations—American Treatment of Black and Red Races—Character of the Carolinians— Slave-Dealers and Slave-Breeders—Conduct of Carolinian Ladies to Negro Slaves—Atrocities of Carolinian Planters.

As we proceeded further up the country, the ground, although still elevated only about twenty or thirty feet above the sea-level, swelled here and there into gentle undulations, which broke in some measure the monotony of a dead level. The grand and prevailing feature in all American scenery is trees: mostly pine, in this part of the country, interspersed with hard-wood trees of various descriptions, chiefly oak; and these generally have a very venerable appearance, owing to the immense quantities of a kind of creeping moss, hanging from their branches in festoons. A great quantity of this moss is dried and beaten with sticks, when it assumes the appearance of black horse-hair, and is made use of in stuffing chairs, sofas, mattresses, &c. It forms, indeed, a regular trade in Charleston; great quantities being annually shipped for the north.

We passed, in our journey, many fields of cotton. I have a few words to say on this subject, which may be interesting to the people of Britain, who have brought the manufacture of this article to great perfection, and carry it to such an amazing extent.

There are two kinds of cotton cultivated in Carolina: the black-seed, or long-staple, sometimes called sea-island, which grows best on rich low lands, near the coast, and is of a finer quality than can be got in any other part of the world; and the green-seed, or short-staple, called upland, generally, and which goes often in Britain by the name of *Bowed* Georgia: for what reason I know not.

Cotton is usually planted in the month of March, but I have several times witnessed a black frost, as late as the 20th April, which so completely blighted the young cotton plants, then about three or four inches high, that the whole field had to be planted over again; which, of course, caused an exceeding late harvest. The seeds of cotton, which are about the size of peas, but of an oblong shape, are planted (after the ground has been perfectly prepared, of course,) three or four together in one hole, in rows about four feet apart, and the same distance between every hole. Soon after the young plants come up, the weakest are pulled up, leaving one at the distance, as I have said, of every four feet. When full-grown the plant is four or five feet high, with a beautiful blossom, and afterwards a pod about as large as a walnut; this, when ripe, bursts open in three or four divisions, and the cotton then appears. A field of it, in this state, looks very fine. As soon as the cotton is fairly ripe, it is gathered by negroes—men, women, and children—who are generally required to collect a certain quantity each day. They carry a small bag or pocket in front of them, into which they put the pods, as they go along, picking them off the stems. The cotton and seeds adhere together, so that it takes about four pounds of pods thus collected to produce one pound of clean cotton. The Sea-island cotton is very easily cleaned; the wool being stripped off the seed, readily and smoothly, by means of two rollers about an inch in diameter, moving in opposite directions, and driven by a treddle, like the wheel of a lathe. The green seed, however, adheres most tenaciously to the wool, and until a machine was invented, some fifty years ago, the planters were at great trouble and expense in cleaning their cotton. The machine to which I allude, is called the cotton-gin, and was invented by a person of the name of Eli Whitney, who, at the time, was tutor in a gentleman's family, in Georgia. After many trials it was brought to perfection; but Mr. Whitney, like many other mechanical inventors and benefactors of mankind, was very unhandsomely treated by those who reaped the benefit of his labours. Before his death, however, he received some very considerable compensation for his invention. The principal part of the cotton-gin, consists of a roller six or eight inches in diameter, and about three feet long, upon which are fastened forty or fifty small circular saws, which turn round in a frame furnished with as many crevices or grooves as there are saws. In front of these chinks is a small trough, into which the cotton and seeds, as they come from the bush, are placed; and as the roller turns round, the *cotton* is drawn through the chinks by means of the teeth of the saws, leaving the seeds in the small trough. At the under side of the row of saws, another roller is placed, and upon this roller a number of strong brushes, made of stout bristles, are fastened, corresponding in number and position to the small saws, and turning in an opposite direction, with many times the velocity of the saw-roller. This, consequently, sweeps the wool clean from off the teeth of the saws, thereby causing them, as they turn to the upper side, to be ready again to seize a fresh quantity from out the trough or feeder. This machine is set in motion by human labour, or by horse power; and it is really a most ingenious piece of mechanism.

In the low country of Carolina, an immense quantity of rice is grown. In some parts of the world, this grain is, I am aware, cultivated upon hills or rising grounds; but in Carolina it requires to be done upon a perfect level, so that the field may be occasionally overflowed with water, to the depth of a few inches; which is done for the purpose of destroying weeds. Under the influence of a powerful sun, this practice naturally produces what is called marsh miasma, which engenders fevers of a dangerous nature: fatal, indeed, to white men in most cases; and even negroes, in some seasons, suffer greatly from it.

Europeans have scarcely any idea of the low lands

of Carolina. What would they think of travelling through endless and almost impervious woods, where the air is in a state of stagnation; and where, in some seasons, stagnant water lies upon the ground in most parts to the depth of twelve or eighteen inches? Even so early as the month of April, I have been in a part of the country about fifteen miles south-west of Charleston, and observed that in driving along the public road, where it led through a swamp, the white passengers in a carriage were obliged to apply a handkerchief to their noses, so noxious and intolerable was the effluvium.

Carolina will continue to suffer from periodical fevers until the low countryis cleared of trees, the swamps drained, the present system of rice-planting put an end to, and the country generally cultivated. All this can only be effected through the instrumentality of negroes; and, as I shall hereafter show, it *may* be done in the course of years by *free* negroes; but never under the system of hopeless slavery.

I may here observe that the whole of the land yet cultivated in Carolina is trifling in proportion to its extent. South Carolina contains nearly 28,000 square miles, or nearly the same extent as Scotland; and the population, white and black, bond and free, is not much over 600,000. Of these there are yet a few thousands of native Indian Americans; but the white man is fast driving these aboriginal proprietors of the soil to the far West; and in a few years hence a native Indian will be a rarity on the east of the Mississippi.

The Americans excuse themselves for their treatment of the Indians, by alleging that as the Indians do not cultivate the soil, it therefore belongs to those who will. The American Government annually pays several hundred thousands of dollars to certain Indian tribes, as compensation-money; but the " truck system," as it is called in England, is in operation, and the poor simple Indians are paid in blankets, muskets, gun-powder, fire-water, &c., at a profit of 200 or 300 per cent. The Americans bind themselves to pay great part of the Indian pension-money *for ever;* but I rather guess that Jonathan will take it into his head to *repudiate* on this score, long before the end of the present century. But indeed it is thought by many judicious men, that ere that period elapses there will be very few of the red men left to trouble their white oppressors.

It was never my fortune to fall in with many Indians together; I have only seen a few stragglers, who come to Charleston now and then; and these (with the exception of a few chiefs, who have occasionally visited the city on their way to see their " great father" at Washington) were by no means *fair samples* of their countrymen. Going about from one grog-shop to another, both men and women were usually in a state of oblivion from the time they entered Charleston, until their departure. Some of the chiefs I have seen were very noble-looking men, and wore splendid and gaudy dresses. The Indians, by-the-by, affect to look upon the negro race with sovereign contempt.

I shall now return to the city, and take the liberty of passing a few remarks on the moral character of the Carolinians. Should these remarks ever reach the eye of a Carolinian, he will probably, without thinking, exclaim, " What, you neegur! do you presume to animadvert upon the character of free-born Republicans? You stab us in the dark, you black rascal! Come forward in open day and let us know your name, and what you are, and we shall soon refute the scandalous lies which you dare to tell about us, while you remain hidden in your hole like a venomous spider." " Yes, massa! Just so. Hear the poor black fellow one word. Let me share the privileges which, as a freeman, you possess yourself; and grant me a safe conduct to any public place in Carolina, or any of the slave states. Guarantee to me protection from all violence to my person, or damage to my property; and last, though not least, grant me the privilege of the *public press*, and I am ready to come forward. But until you do this, I shall remain unknown, and take the advantage of spreading the *truth* in regard to slavery and all that pertains to it, by means of the British press; which it is beyond your power to control."

The Carolinians have been described by some of their northern brethren as proud, overbearing, quick-tempered men; exceedingly vain, extravagant, licentious, and fond of gambling; but, at the same time, hospitable, generous, warm-hearted, and not without animal courage. I shall not attempt to analyze their characters, or reconcile seeming contradictions, but will be content to relate a few anecdotes.

I will allow that, during the season of sickness, the people of Charleston have, again and again, displayed much kindness and sympathy to strangers; both in regard to the opening of their purse, and personal attention. I have known ladies of delicacy and refinement go from house to house, administering to the wants of the distressed with their own hands; and in the event of fire (which, as already observed, is a very frequent disaster here), their generosity has, in many instances, been most nobly displayed towards the sufferers. In their domestic virtues also, in many instances, both male and female Carolinians are beautiful examples of love and unity; and in some families their kindness and sympathy extends even to their black dependants: white ladies, with their own hands, administering medicine and cordials to the sick negroes. Perhaps some English abolitionist may observe, " Oh! they were afraid of their property; it was no genuine pity for their negro, but merely the fear that death would deprive them of so many hundred dollars." This consideration might operate a little, but in most cases, I am convinced, that the true milk of human kindness prompted them to these labours of love. I could expatiate at considerable length upon the acquirements, and the natural virtues of the ladies of Carolina in general, and I have pleasure in bearing testimony to their many amiable qualities; and also, as far as a man of my colour may be permitted to judge, as to their personal beauty. But with all this there is still this one " damning spot," to disfigure and blot out many virtues: viz., their cruel prejudice against, and too oft cruel treatment of, black people. To their honour, however, I must repeat the remark that I have often heard made here, that there has hardly ever been a single case of a native-born white lady of Charleston descending so low as to join the degraded class of " women of the town." These unhappy creatures come down in crowds from the northern cities at the commencement of every winter, and return on the approach of the sickly season. It is, however, neither my province nor my desire to enlarge on this subject.

The love of money, that " root of all evil," often leads men in this place, who are, otherwise, possessed of sense and feeling, to do many things derogatory to their characters, and very humiliating to contemplate. I knew one old gentleman who owned property to the amount of half a million dollars, and who, nevertheless, for many years, had a peculiar satisfaction in purchasing at Vendue what he called " bargains," or " job lots," in the shape of negro women. These he would take home to his wife, an old Scotch lady, and, under her instructions, they became, in a few years, servants of the first class—as cooks or laundresses; and when they had been thus accomplished, old Mr. Lamp carried them down again to Vendue, and there they were sure to command large prices, in the proportion of at least three to one for his outlaid money. " Mr. Lamp! Mr. Lamp!" his old wife would ex-

Q

claim, "really it is most annoying that I have no sooner got proper cooks than off you hurry them to auction." "Well, well, my dear! you know you are a very clever woman, and you would tire for want of employment if I did not oblige you in this way. I shall try and get you a fresh young girl or two next week, so say no more about it. You see it is always turning over a few hundred dollars."

I was also acquainted with a Mr. Dunnam, a boot and shoe maker, who made a regular traffic of breeding negroes, and had hardly ever less than fifteen or twenty negro children swarming in his back yard. He was a shrewd judge of the value of this peculiar kind of property. I remember his purchasing a negro girl, named Sally, about twenty years of age, with a child at her breast, in the year 1811, when prices were dull, for 350 dollars only. Sally soon found a husband among Mr. Dunnam's shoemakers; and by the year 1818, Sally had become the mother of five fine children; when as negroes were then selling at an extravagant price in consequence of the very high rates of cotton and rice, the knowing boot-maker brought the whole family to the Vendue table. I witnessed the sale personally, and can assure the reader that they brought 530 dollars a head, or, in all, 3180 dollars! Such enormous profits on the *raising* of negroes certainly offer a great temptation to men whose god is money.

It is still more to be deplored, that the love of money should operate so powerfully upon the mind of woman, as to destroy that natural delicacy of feeling which is one of the brightest ornaments of the softer sex. I was standing one day at the door of a grocery, in East Bay Street, when two white ladies, finely dressed, walking on the pavement, came up while a young black woman was conversing with me; the elder of the ladies stopped, and, drawing my female friend aside, asked her to whom she belonged. "I belong to nobody, ma'am," said the young woman, dropping a courtesy; "I do be free woman, ma'am." "Oh! very well, my good girl—never mind; I only thought you looked as if you would *breed* well!" The white *ladies* then went on their way. Is any comment here necessary?

I will just give one or two more examples. "But how did you become acquainted with these private scenes, Mr. Zamba?" some reader may ask. "Some of them through the intervention of Zillah; who, like the rest of her sex, was fond of a bit of gossip with her sister waiting-maids." One of these told her that when waiting on her young mistress, a Miss Treuman, in her bed-chamber, where also one or two of the young lady's sisters were present, Miss Treuman would lean back in her chair and say, "Now Dinah, come hither and rub my legs." Dinah forthwith kneeled down on the floor; and having pulled off the young lady's stockings, commenced in as gentle a manner as possible to manipulate the limbs of this Carolinian beauty for she really *was* a beauty: at least in outward appearance. "Rub a little harder now, Dinah; ah! that's a good wench, just so: ah! that'll do. Now, you black devil, have you scratched

me ?   If you scratch me as much as a pin's point I
shall have you regularly cowskinned in the morning."
" Beg pardon, missy," said poor Dinah, " I not
scratch missy legs for de world." — " Well, just be
careful now, wench, for you know that there is venom
beneath the nails of you black heathens." When
Zillah related this little incident to me, I could not
but laugh ; and I have since wondered much whether
duchesses and countesses in England cause their waiting-maids to rub *their* legs before going to bed.

I have a more serious tale now, however, to relate.
I was taken by my master one day to assist in serving at a large dinner-party, at which he was a guest.
As the chief servant of the house was carrying into
the dining-room a large crystal epergne, loaded with
jellies, custards, syllabubs, &c., he most unfortunately
stumbled, and the whole concern was smashed to
pieces. I could observe all that passed, as I was
at the moment standing at the sideboard ; and poor
Tom was by no means to blame, for the large epergne
that he carried prevented his seeing a stool which
one of the host's children had left in the way. The
gentleman of the house was a very fine man, and
attempted to pass off the matter with a laugh ; but
I could observe the mistress of the house turn pale
as a corpse, whilst her eyes flashed like those of a
tigress : though in a short time she appeared more
composed, and all went on quietly until the guests
retired. I learned, however, that no sooner was the
house clear of strangers than Mrs. Alderton made her
appearance in the kitchen—where poor Tom, assisted

by his fellow-servants, was busily employed in cleaning and clearing away matters—and broke out most furiously. " You abominable, infamous neegur! to break my epergne, which cost ninety dollars. But you shall pay for it, you black brute you." And here she attacked poor Tom with a pair of iron tongs, laying on with all her might and regardless of where she struck him. She would most probably have put it out of Tom's power to break any more crystals in this world, had not her husband interfered. Nothing, however, could ever pacify this vindictive lady ; and after Tom had endured for some months the most brutal usage, his master, for peace's sake, and out of humanity, sent him to the Vendue table.

I feel no pleasure in recording such savage cruelties perpetrated by the white ladies of Carolina ; but truth ought not to be concealed, if the making known of that truth should in any way hereafter tend to ameliorate the unhappy condition of domestic slaves. Nor can I pass over the opinions and sentiments of a young lady of Charleston, in regard to the punishment of negroes at the time of the insurrection in 1822. Her father, a Mr. Wiggins, being one of the city authorities, his opinion had considerable influence. One morning, at the time of the trials, as Mr. Wiggins rose from breakfast, Miss Lydia followed him to the door and said, " Dear pa, I tell you what you should do with these horrible wretches of negroes, who designed to murder us all. I would have a large brander (gridiron) made, pa, and chain every soul of them upon it, and then kindle a fire underneath. Do you not think it an excellent plan, pa? Do recommend it to the judges." Mr. Wiggins, who had more humane feelings within his breast than his delicate and lovely daughter, replied, " Hush! hush! Liddy; you are going too far. I don't like to hear such talk from *you*; it does not become you at all. Go to your room quickly, and read your bible." This fair daughter of the American Republic—accomplished, refined, and elegant—who would have turned aside to avoid treading upon a worm, utters in cold blood a proposal which the Inquisition, in the height of its power, could hardly have surpassed! This is only another proof that the existence of slavery, in any country, debases and degrades the oppressor, in a moral sense, even more than it does the poor trembling slave.

I might fill a large volume with the deliberate murders, rapes, and other outrages upon humanity, which have been practised by Carolinians and other slaveholders against their helpless victims; but I will only give an instance or two. A Mr. Wilkins kept an inn, within twenty miles of Charleston, who was a wealthy man and fond enough of money; but when his passions obtained the mastery over him— and that was every day, almost every hour—he acted more like an incarnate devil than a human being. It was well known to many—indeed it was a matter of public notoriety—that he had killed several of his slaves, by usage of the most revolting nature. On one occasion it happened, that having stripped two of his slaves—one of them a woman—nearly naked, he lashed them ferociously with a horsewhip; to escape from this cruel chastisement they broke loose from him, and making for a wooden bridge which was within a hundred yards of the house, leaped into the river and were speedily drowned, or devoured by the alligators. Their inhuman persecutor, thinking only of his loss, said, " D— them! but I gave them a handsome walloping first! They may go to hell! I don't mind a few hundred dollars, when I get satisfaction for it."

About ten miles from town, one Captain Gullan had an estate, upon which were about fifty negroes; and amongst them was a very handsome young married woman, named Juno, who had taken the captain's fancy: and he, too, be it observed, was a married man. The captain had first attempted, by what his brother white men here call *fair means*—that is, by the offer of a little favour or indulgence, or a few dollars—to seduce poor Juno; but she resisted all the overtures of the white libertine. The captain, however, would not be thus repelled, but persecuted her from day to day. One evening, after her field-task was over, he paid her a visit in her little hut; her husband being present, and their only child, an infant. " Juno, I wish to see you this evening at the house," said the captain; " you will call up after dark. My wife is in town at present, and I wish you to come particularly; so do not disappoint me, or, by the Lord! I shall make it a bad business for both you and Billy here." Poor Billy sat apart, and never opened his lips; but Juno, clasping her hands

together, said, imploringly—" Do, dear massa, excuse me—do, for God's sake, excuse me. I know
you want me for no good. Oh! dear massa, haven't
you a dear, sweet, good lady of your own? Why
will you take trouble for a poor negro woman? I
will serve you night and day: but do not ask me
to be faithless to my poor Billy."—" Hold your jaw
now, you neegur," said he, " and give me none of
your sermons. Come up as I bid you." But Juno
held out, and did not go to the house. So the following day Captain Gullan came down on horseback
to Juno's hut, early in the morning, just as the
negroes were standing at their doors, preparing to go
to their task in the field. He called out, and the
woman came to the door with her husband. "Come
this way, Juno," said the captain, and whispered something in her ear. At this the poor woman renewed
her supplications that he would let her alone. "Take
that, then, you d—d neegur," said he—" and that"
cutting her over the head and shoulders with his
horse-whip. " By God! I shall make you obey
me." Billy rushed between his wife and her brutal
assailant, holding up his hands to ward off the blows
from her, and crying out—" Do, for God's sake,
massa, let us do our work in peace, and let poor
Juno alone!"—" Do you dare to lift up your hands
and attempt to resist me, you infernal black dog?"
said the captain. " Take that, and be d—d;" and
he drew a pistol from his pocket, and shot poor Billy
through the heart. The whole of the negroes around,
at this horrible deed, set up a shout of horror; and,

as chance would have it, at this moment two of the
neighbouring planters made their appearance quite
unexpectedly. " Why, captain," said one of them,
" what is all this ? You really have gone too far, I
expect;" and stooping down to the now dead negro,
he added, " why, you have killed one of your best
negroes! God bless me, captain, do you know what
you have done ?"—" Done !" said the murderer,
quite coolly ; " yes, I know what I have done. Do
you think I would allow a cursed negro to lift his
hand to me, and not make him pay for it ? I was
only acting in self-defence."—" Massa! massa !"
exclaimed some of the negroes, " poor Bill only held
up his hands to save Juno."—" Peace! you confounded rascals," cried the captain; and riding
amongst them, he struck right and left with his
whip, and dispersed them. He then returned to his
two white neighbours, and said—" Did not both of
you see that black rascal with his hands uplifted to
me before you came forward ?"—" Why, captain, I
believe I did see him with his hands up," said one;
"but I question if it was to strike you. I think you have
been too rash ; and I can tell you, captain, that I do
not envy your position any how." The captain then
threw down a few dollars on the ground, and said to
the poor bereaved widow—" There, Juno, you may
tell the gang that no work need be done to-day.
You can send for some rum to treat them, and get
Bill buried." He seemed a *little* softened ; but he
rode back to his own house with his two friends, and
no more was heard of the matter. This *murder*, like

many others perpetrated on black people in Carolina, remains unpunished to this day.

The humane reader will now probably inquire— " Is there no law to punish a white man who *deliberately* murders a negro ?" I answer that I have heard some *talk* of such a law existing in Carolina, which awards the punishment of death in such cases; but I boldly ask, and without fear of contradiction, " Has it ever been known in Carolina that a white man was brought to the gallows for murdering a black ?" It cannot be denied that hundreds, nay thousands, of such murders have actually been committed. But how is the murderer to be convicted? When a white man deliberately murders a black, he takes especial care that he does not do so in the presence of a white man; but should he commit the crime before ten thousand blacks, *their* evidence is of no avail. I may even add, that the murder of negroes is actually permitted by *law;* for I have Charleston papers in my possession in which there are advertisements by white slave-owners, offering a reward for a certain runaway negro, in these words— " *Ten* dollars will be given to any person bringing the said runaway alive to the subscriber; or, *one hundred* dollars for his *head.*" If this be not murder, what is it ? And though it may not be directly sanctioned by law, the practice is too common and open to be considered illegal.

CHAPTER XIV.

Negro conspiracies against the Whites—anecdotes of Negroes.

While speaking of such dreadful subjects, I may as well in this place say a few words regarding the negro conspiracy which came to light in 1822. Like almost all conspiracies, it was discovered by one of the conspirators themselves; from whose evidence (for the evidence of a black man against individuals of his own colour, is quite valid in *law* here) it appeared that on a certain Sabbath afternoon, as soon as the bells commenced ringing for church, the whole of the conspirators, who expected to be joined by every able black man in the city, were to commence a massacre of every white male in the city, leaving the white ladies as partners to the conquerors. It was also said that every black female was to be murdered at the same time: but this, I conceive, however, to have been an invention of the white men, so as to cast more odium on the conspiracy. One thing is certain, that I had no notion of this affair; my black brethren knew that I was well enough off, and, of course, never thought of dragging me into the business. The man who informed on his fellow-conspirators, did so, on account of his master, it was said: he wished to have his master exempted from the general slaughter; but his comrades, not consenting to this, he, out of gratitude for former kindness, "peached." The conspirators had been in the habit of meeting in a certain place in King Street, where they concocted their plans, and initiated new members, with many strange oaths and ceremonies. The leading men in this conspiracy were mostly mulattoes, men of talent and education; and who, in any other country, would have been hailed as patriots. I must allow that their schemes were most bloody and savage: but what could be expected under such oppression and tyranny. On a certain day they were arrested, to the number of several hundreds, in a most quiet and cautious manner: with hardly any stir indeed. The most of them were legally (in a nominal sense) tried, a great number convicted, and about forty were hanged: twenty-two on one gallows, the first day, and a few now and then immediately thereafter. They all exhibited much courage and calmness at the last; and several, with the rope round their necks, addressed their fellow blacks who were present, beseeching them to be true to the cause of freedom, and never to cease conspiring against their white tyrants, until their purpose would be accomplished, which it sooner

or later could not fail to be.   Two of the most
noted who suffered, were named Telemaque Vesey
(commonly called Denmark Vesey) and Gullah
Jack (Angola Jack).   Denmark was a very clever
and accomplished fellow.   Four negroes were re-
spited on one of the execution-days at the scaffold,
and received a solemn promise that their lives would
be spared, provided they made a full confession;
but after they had confessed, it was decided by
their white masters, that the things which they had
divulged were of such a dreadful nature, and so
deeply implicated these negroes, that they were unfit
to live; so, a few days afterwards, they were again
taken out and executed.   This signal proof of the
bad faith of the white men of Carolina, will not
soon be forgotten by the negroes.

Since that period, several conspiracies of a less
extensive character have come to light; and there
is little doubt, that, although the flame of liberty
is for the present smothered: it will break out some
day with a fearful explosion, unless, indeed, some
conciliatory measures are resorted to in behalf of
the oppressed negro.   For my own part, I most
earnestly deprecate having recourse to physical force;
and I hope to make it clear, (that unless the whites
should be for ever blind to their own interests)
slavery may be totally abolished in the United
States, in a gradual and unobjectionable manner;
without detriment to any one, and so as to secure
happiness, honour, and security to all, both black
and white.

I will now relate an anecdote or two of a more pleasing nature. I mentioned in a former part, that black people were compelled to give way in the streets for a white, even of the lowest and most degraded class. There was an elderly white man, a very ill-tempered fellow, who walked about a good deal, and took a peculiar delight in chastising any unfortunate coloured person he met with, who did not instantly get out of his way. He always carried a huge stick over his shoulder, and whenever he met with a negro, male or female, who did not in a twinkling scamper off the pavement, down came the cudgel upon their crown with right good will. Now there was a negro carpenter, a big jolly fellow, with whom this spiteful old white man came in contact several times; and as the big carpenter did not so readily make way as the old gentleman thought proper, he applied his stick more than once to the jolly carpenter's upper story: or at least aimed at him. It happened that the carpenter met his white enemy almost every morning at the breakfast hour, in a retired part at the north end of East Bay Street; so one morning he watched cautiously, and although there were black people in plenty within view, by good luck there was not a solitary white. There had been a good deal of rain previously, and the middle of the street was a perfect puddle; so when the carpenter came near his old friend, he stept off the footpath, and then turning quietly round, he lifted the old fellow by the neck and the heels, as one would do an infant, and, carrying him delibe-

rately over to the deepest part of the puddle, softly
and cautiously laid him down upon his back in it,
and then took to his heels.   Either through fear
or policy, or perhaps from a feeling that he had
been acting too much the tyrant, the redoubtable
white man with the cudgel was much more cautious
and peaceable in his walk thereafter; and Big Bob
the carpenter, was much applauded by all his
coloured acquaintances, and even many white gentlemen laughed at the exploit.

Let me relate another anecdote, in which I was one
of the actors myself.   I was sent, one day, to the store
of a Mr. Landen, to arrange some goods which were
to be sold by auction in one of the floors of a large
building; and I was assisted in performing this duty
by a fine negro lad, of about fifteen, named Peter.
While Peter was employed in turning over some
boxes of muslin, a young white gentleman (oh, how
much is this word misapplied and abused in every-
day life!) entered, and, going up to Peter, gave him
a switch over the back with a cane, saying, " You
blasted neegur! is that the way to place a box—with
the marked end down?"   Peter looked up, and said,
" Stop, Massa Halsey; you always abusing me for
nothing.   I shall tell Mr. Landen."—" Tell the d—l,
you black thief!" retorted Halsey; again attacking
poor Peter, who made his escape behind some bales.
A chase commenced, the white youth giving Peter
a blow as often as he could reach him; at length
the poor negro, bursting into tears, exclaimed, " My
God! if I were but white for one half hour, I would

repay you, Massa Halsey." This only exasperated the white gentleman still more, and I could refrain no longer. Being aware that all the clerks were up stairs, I went and shut the door, and coming up to Mr. Halsey, said, in a firm voice, " I tell you what, young gentleman, you are very wrong to strike that poor boy, and it shows you are a coward at heart; for you know well that he dare not return your blows unless at the peril of losing his right hand." At this the young white puppy lifted his cane, as if to strike me; but I stopped him by saying, " Now, Mr. Halsey, take care what you are about; I am Mr. Naylor's property, and if you do strike me, you shall pay dearly for it. And now, as there are no white people to witness against me, I shall give you a lesson for once." So saying, I seized him by the shoulders (I did not strike him), and *shook* him so very heartily— for I was a pretty stout fellow at that time—that, when he could get breath, he whined and prayed for mercy. At last I desisted, and taking him in my arms, placed him gently upon a bale of carpeting, to recover his wind and compose himself. He was so ashamed and crest-fallen, that I don't think he ever mentioned the story to any one.

Although the blacks are looked down upon with so much contempt in general, yet I have seen at least one instance, where the talents of a negro were brought into public requisition; no less an honour being conferred upon him than " Master of Ceremonies" at a grand ball given by the St. Andrew's Society, which numbered among its members many

of the first merchants in the city. I accompanied
my master thither, and was allowed occasionally to
peep in at the door. The ball was held in a splendid
hall, well lighted up, and the floor was chalked at an
expense of thirty dollars. The American eagle, surrounded by stars (I really forget whether the stripes
were depicted or not) and other ornaments, formed
the centre; and all around it the Scottish thistle displayed its prickly beard. There was a great assem-
blage of *beauty and fashion,* sprinkled with a little
republican pride and arrogance; but the principal object of attraction to me was old Joe, the master of
the ceremonies. Joe was a complete negro—none of
your half-and-half breed, but a genuine son of
Africa. He was nearly sixty years of age, but still
an erect, handsome-looking fellow; and he was
dressed in white kerseymere breeches, white silk
stockings, a white vest, and blue coat with gilt buttons: his feet were cased in red morocco pumps, and
his hair, which required no curling-irons, was well
powdered. He displayed a flashy gold chain round
his neck, and at his watch hung half a dozen large
seals; whilst an elegant silver-topped cane was his
wand of office. Joe stood in great dignity at the
end of the room, and arranged the whole business of
the evening—placing the dancers in their proper stations, directing the musicians, introducing ladies and
gentlemen to each other; and, in fact, as I was informed by people more versant in high life than
myself, performing the character he represented with
credit to himself, and satisfaction to all concerned.

R

It was curious to see Joe stamping with his foot, and bawling out, " Now, Missy Foot, this way if you please; right hand to Massa Starky, cross over den, and sachee dere. Now, Missy Lemman, hands across, and set to Massa Suydam." Long before the ball was finished, the feet of the dancers had quite oblite-rated the American eagle; but the Scottish thistle still remained, to the evident satisfaction of some hot-blooded republicans. I thought to myself, that by granting to negroes more liberty, and more indul-gence in trifling matters, the whites would more securely bind them to allegiance than by everlasting oppression.

I will now relate a couple of anecdotes that will, I hope, reflect honour upon the black race, and no discredit to the white persons concerned. There was an elderly Scotsman who kept a small grocery store in Market-street, and carried on considerable traffic with black people. He had been formerly very ex-tensively engaged in commerce, but had met with many misfortunes; and to add to his mishaps, he was attacked by a slow fever, in the summer of 1809. He struggled against it as long as he could, and having no assistant in his little business, at last be-came so weak, that he could not rise from bed to take off the shutters from his windows. In this emergency, without a white friend to help him, a negro woman, named Hagar, who kept a stall for kitchen herbs in the market, opposite the Scotsman's door, and who had often bought and sold with him, came, like a good Samaritan, to his aid: she made the sick stranger's bed, cooked any little victuals he could take, made gruel and other messes for him, and gave him herb drinks of her own composition as medicine. She nursed and attended upon him several hours every day for about six weeks, and at length had the satisfaction to see her patient once more get up and open his own windows. Some years afterwards this Scotsman had a large business going on in the foreign trade, and was greatly elevated above the rank of a grocer; but he never passed through the market without stopping to say a few words to old Hagar, and many a little present did he give her.

One Sabbath afternoon I was walking through Boundary-street, in the upper part of the city, and perceived thirty or forty boys and young men, of all colours, gathered together at one side of the street, and occasionally shouting and laughing. On coming closer I discovered a white man, dressed in light clothing, such as mechanics generally wear, sitting on the ground. He was very much intoxicated, and had tripped over a hillock of rubbish, in which were some broken bottles, and was severely cut about the legs and ankles, which were bleeding profusely. Just at the moment I got into the crowd, he was stooping his head down, and *sucking* one of his ankles, repeating to himself " American blood for ever will reign, you d——d rascals!" He then looked up to those who surrounded him, with his face besmeared with blood and dust, like his clothes. I had seldom seen such a revolting picture of intoxication. I felt much

for the poor man, but was quite at a loss how to assist
him; when at this moment an old negro man and his
wife came out from a small wooden house adjacent,
and upon learning what was the matter exclaimed,
" Poor buckrah! Gar Amighty! he die there—he
bleed to death. Come, boy," said he to me, " help
me to carry the poor man, and I shall give him a
corner to lie down, till he get sober."   I was quite
glad to hear the old man say so, and turning to some
of the negro boys, I said, " Now, my boys, I would
advise you to be off, as fast as you like, or I shall
give one or two of you something that you will not
like; and, as for you, young gentlemen," said I, turning to the lordly part of the mob, " 1 hope you will
leave the poor man. I should think that you have
been sufficiently amused for one Sunday afternoon."
The biggest boys muttered something about " black
rascals," but dispersed speedily. We now had the
drunken and bleeding man conveyed to old Jacob's
dwelling, and I assisted in washing the poor fellow,
and managed to bind up his wounds. As soon as he
came a little to himself, he seemed quite cast down,
and muttered many thanks. " Who the devil would
have expected this from niggers?" said he to himself. " Well, anyhow, I shall likely be better to-
morrow; and they shant lose by it."   In the mean
time, old Mary made a cup of coffee for their guest;
and pointing out a mattress on the floor of a small
closet, their only other apartment, said that buckrah
would be welcome to stay till the morning. I then
left them, saying, I would call next day. I did so,

after breakfast, and found that the white man had been down at his lodging, and had returned in a better dress, and to show his gratitude, he handed the old couple ten silver dollars. Old Isaac refused to take them at first, and said he did such things for the love of God, and would find his reward hereafter; but the white man insisted, and old Isaac put the coins in his pocket, saying, " Very useful things, them same dollars; don't find them every day. Many thanks to you, massa buckrah!" The man was a carpenter, doing a pretty good piece of business, not an habitual drunkard; but had fallen in with some rascals at a tavern, who he believed had put poison in his drink, as he had never in his life been so overtaken before,—and I often saw him afterwards. Old Isaac sold a few hucksteries in his little dwelling, and he told me, " Old Mary and self contrived to live somehow; God only knows how, sometimes." I had the satisfaction, without detriment to myself, to assist him somewhat in his little trade, by advancing a few dollars; and the grateful carpenter called upon him repeatedly, and never did so without bringing some little present in his pocket for old Mary. Such incidents reflect honour on human nature; and sure am I, that I have as much pleasure in recording the virtues, or amiable points of character in the white race, as in my own.

CHAPTER XV.

Zamba's Plan for the Gradual Extinction of Negro Slavery in the United States.—Advantages of Free over Slave Labour.—Dangers from the Separation of Free and Slave States.—Zamba's Appeal to the British Nation.—Conclusion.

I CANNOT better conclude this narrative than by submitting certain propositions to the General Government of the United States; and, if facts and figures carry any weight with them, those whom I take· the liberty of addressing must be wilfully and obstinately blind to common sense and justice should they not admit that, at least, my arguments are sound.

I would observe, in the first place, then (although I am aware that it will be displeasing to many honest abolitionists both in Britain and America, and also to many of my black brethren), that emancipation should be gradual, both for the sake of master and slave. It may be urged that Britain granted freedom all at once to the slaves in her colonies; but it must be borne in mind that many thousands of these slaves had had the benefit of education for many years previously; and, further, that the few years of apprenticeship served as a kind of modification between abject slavery and absolute freedom. I mean that, in some measure, it prevented any ill consequences arising from too sudden a change in the condition of so many thousands of men. I am aware, while addressing the General Congress of the United States, that it is not in their power to emancipate the slaves of Carolina or Georgia, as the laws of each State can only be altered by its own individual legislature. But I will suggest a very simple plan, by following out which, negro emancipation may be gradually, yet certainly, brought about. I hardly know whether it ought to be matter of joy or grief to abolitionists, that the General Congress has lately shown its determination to perpetuate slavery more than ever. I understand that it lately passed a bill declaring that no petitions in favour of abolition would be allowed to be placed on the table of the House of Representatives; and further, in admitting Florida lately as a new State, it was on the express condition that the State of Florida should at *no future period* grant emancipation to her slaves. Now that the states are about including Texas in the Union, and stretching out their hand towards Oregon, they will no doubt stipulate for the same conditions. How it is that the anti-freedom party have obtained such an ascendency in the House, I know not. Do the white men of America really imagine that the black race will *never* obtain their just rights? that they will *for ever* submit to be oppressed and trampled upon? The negroes of America are rapidly increasing in numbers; the present slave population of the United States may be reckoned at 2,800,000, and the free black population at 600,000. A large proportion of able-bodied men are included in this number—men who, by a very little discipline and with proper arms, would be found no contemptible soldiers; and who, if once aroused in the cause of personal freedom, would lay down their arms only with their lives. Such a number of robust men, brooding under a sense of the wrongs inflicted on them for a long series of years, residing in the heart of any commonwealth, and with so many opportunities of retaliating upon their oppressors in case of an invasion, is not to be contemplated without apprehension. For my own part, I am most decidedly opposed to all physical force;—but what is the opinion of one, or a few, to that of millions of my oppressed race?

During the last war with Britain, there were not twenty negroes in Charleston but were daily praying that John Bull would land and chastise their proud masters; and they were ready, to a man, with such arms as they could command, to turn against their oppressors.

But it is in the power of the Americans to convert the whole of their black population into staunch and determined defenders of the land in which they live; instead of being, as they necessarily must be under the present state of things, doubtful and suspicious *neutrals*, at the best, if not covert enemies.

I shall now, with all deference, propose a plan, by which the whole of the slaves in the United States

may be emancipated, with honour to the whites, and
without detriment to their purses, in the course of
twenty-one or thirty years. Congress cannot interfere with the individual laws of any particular State
of the Union, and emancipate the negroes of that
State; but it can pass a law, imposing a tax. Now
a tax of five dollars per head, annually, on every
coloured person in America, *whether bond or free,*
would effect this happy change in twenty-one years;
or, a tax of only three dollars, would bring it about in
thirty years. At the rate of five dollars per head,
allowing the money to yield 6 per cent., and calculating compound interest (and there is no doubt but
that in a thriving, enterprising, and rapidly increasing
country, as America undoubtedly is, money can be
safely invested, so as to make my calculations good,)
a five dollar poll-tax on negroes, would produce in
twenty-one years, 670,000,000 dollars. But to make
the tax easier to the planters, who must pay for their
slaves, and to give more time for the gradual ameli-
oration of the negro's moral condition, I shall go upon
the three dollar tax.

But, in postponing emancipation for the long period
of thirty years, many of my brother blacks may say,
" Ay, it is well enough for you, Zamba, to talk in
this easy way—you who have never fully known the
wretchedness of slavery; but for us, to look forward
for thirty years, is dreadful." I allow it is a long
period; but such important changes generally require
time. Should any abolitionist, black or white, pro-

pose a more speedy and rational plan, I shall indeed feel happy.

There is no planter who owns one hundred negroes, but can easily manage to pay a tax of three hundred dollars per annum; especially if he reflects what a boon it will confer on millions of oppressed fellow-creatures; and finally, that it will all *revert to him threefold*. As for the *free* coloured people in the United States, there are but few of them who could not afford three dollars per annum, in such a good cause; and those who are really very indigent will have the emancipation tax paid by some charitable brother, who will do thus much for the sake of his enslaved brethren. I am convinced, also, that there are thousands of white abolitionists in America, who would cheerfully, were such a plan in operation, contribute their mite, and see that the tax would be forthcoming for the poorest coloured person in the land. And were an appeal made to the negroes' friends in other countries, there would be many thousands of dollars sent annually from the abolitionists of Britain, to assist in the good work. Independent of all extraneous aid, however, I calculate that three dollars per head per annum, would, in the first year, yield about ten millions of dollars, at 6 per cent.; and compound interest on this sum, and on ten millions additional every year, for thirty years, would at the end of that period amount altogether to eight hundred and forty-five millions of dollars; or two hundred and fifty-three dollars per head, *compensa-*

tion money, for each negro slave—man, woman, and child,—in the whole of the United States of America. This would be *more* than *double* the amount of compensation money given to the planters in the British Colonies, for emancipating their slaves : the average paid them for 800,000 slaves was twenty-five pounds, or one hundred and ten dollars per head.

I have made my foregoing calculations in *round* numbers, but am very near the truth. It will be seen that the whole amount to be paid out as tax, in thirty years, for each negro, would only amount to ninety dollars, and for this, at the end of the thirty years, the planter would receive back two hundred and fifty-three dollars, on condition of emancipating his negro. In fact, it would be something similar to the investment of the money in a savings bank. The result would be profitable, and the end attained glorious! It may be urged that the number of negroes, in thirty years, will have greatly increased. So, also, would the annual poll-tax, and consequently the capital and interest; thus the one may go to balance the other. Would it not be a glorious thing, Oh Americans! that on the 4th July 1876—on the *centenary of your own independence*—you should be able to celebrate the independence and liberty of *every living soul* within the precincts of your vast and beautiful dominions?

Were Congress to adopt this plan, I should recommend, that as soon as the law passed, means should be immediately adopted for the education of the negroes. Let a few public schools be established in towns, and a teacher appointed upon every estate in the country, of any consequence. But were the law passed, there is no doubt that the means to effect this desirable object would be forthcoming. I have no ambition to make my fellow-blacks learned men: only enable them to read the Bible, and the blessing of Heaven will second your endeavours. Let emissaries, or missionaries, be sent among the slaves, to explain all that is intended to be done for them, and to show them that much will depend upon their own orderly and peaceable behaviour; and being thus civilized and instructed by degrees, there will be few, indeed, in a state of ignorance, at the end of thirty years. I would answer for my brethren that their industry, and their gratitude, will be developed in proportion as they become enlightened.

I shall now endeavour to show that, after you have emancipated your slaves, you may hire them as free labourers with more advantage to yourselves and them, than under the present system. I believe that on certain estates, for example, the labour of a negro for four days in the week will be amply sufficient; and supposing you hired them at 25 cents per day, that would be 52 dollars per annum. At present you value an able-bodied field negro at 500 dollars; the interest on this sum, at 6 per cent., is 30 dollars; and you cannot clothe and feed him, and pay for a doctor to attend in case of sickness, under 30 dollars per annum at least—making 60 dollars per annum; so that you would save 8 dollars per annum, and have the command of the 500 dollars (the first price or cost of the negro) to extend your plantation, or otherwise, as you chose. Besides, at present you run the risk daily of losing your negro by the hand of death; you must also support him in sickness and in old age: but, by hiring him as a free labourer, you would be free from all this responsibility and loss.

Allow me to lay before you another calculation, which ought to convince any one who is not blindly and determinedly prejudiced, of the reasonableness of my plan. A planter, who at present has 100 negroes on an estate, cannot calculate upon the work of more than one-half, after deducting infants, old people, and women not in condition to labour; but I shall allow that sixty can be reckoned able-bodied. Now, calculate 100 negroes at 300 dollars per head—that is 30,000 dollars; this at 6 per cent. interest, is 1800 dollars. You cannot reckon less than 20 dollars per head for food, clothes, and medical attendance, or 2000 dollars in all; which, with the 1800 above as interest, makes 3800 dollars per annum for the services of 60 labourers. You might hire 60 free labourers at 52 dollars per ann. each, or 3120 dollars in all; thereby saving 680 dollars per annum, and be clear of all the burdens before mentioned.

I am, however, making these calculations on the supposition that the negro be allowed a small plot of ground to raise provisions for himself and family; for there are millions upon millions of acres lying waste in Carolina, which, if cultivated, would render the country much more healthy. Say that every able-bodied negro be allowed five acres; or, where land is not so plenty, two or three acres; by devoting his own two days in the week to the cultivation of his own land, he could raise amply sufficient for all that he and his family can consume; and the wages he receives would provide clothes, education, and all other requisites in abundance. By adopting such measures, you would transform the poor, trembling, heart-broken, hopeless, ignorant, and discontented slave into a free, brave, happy, intelligent, and patriotic peasant—ready at all times to defend his house and his children, and to follow the (then truly free) republican standard of America against every invader.

Then there would be no aspirations or prayers that a foreign enemy might come to their relief; but the free and contented negro would identify himself with the soil of America, and shed his heart's blood in her defence, and in that of his brother freemen, white or black.

Should Congress, however, be blind to the real interests of America, and treat with contempt all proposals which have been or may be made by abolitionists, it will merely hasten the time when a separation of the States will take place. The northern and the southern, or rather the free and the slave-holding States, in their present condition, are an ill-matched pair. The free States, in their alliance with the slave States, are obliged to submit to many disagreeables, merely because they are found in bad company: they have to share all the obloquy due only to slave-holders, without reaping any advantage.

On the other hand, I must allow that it is quite too hard that a Carolinian should have to pay *double*, or perhaps *treble*, price for a piece of British muslin or cotton, merely that manufacturers in the northern States may be aggrandized. Supposing, which is by no means unlikely, that a separation of the States should take place some years hence, how will the slave States then be situated? At present the proportion of whites to blacks, in the whole of the United States, is as 15 to 3; but were the slave States fairly disjoined from the free, then the proportion in these slave States, of white men to the coloured portion, would only be about as 5 or $5\frac{1}{2}$ to 3. Then, in case of a foreign war, would not the danger of the slave States—from the disaffected and discontented members of their *own household*, so to say—be vastly aggravated? And, even in time of peace, would not the free States stand most convenient as a place of refuge to runaway negroes? The editors of the newspapers in Charleston, Savannah, New Orleans, and other cities in the south, daily publish, without thinking of it, gross and glaring libels on their fellow-citizens; for column upon column of their papers are filled with nothing but advertisements for runaway negroes. And, in many cases, such outrages upon the best feelings of human nature appear, as the following :—" Dinah: has a mother residing at such an estate in the country, and a sister at such another place—any white person proving that such have harboured her, will be rewarded, and the parties visited with the *utmost rigour of the law*." Alas, poor

America! alas, poor humanity! A mother, or a sister, must undergo the utmost penalty of the law for protecting their own flesh and blood! Yes! a mother, who endeavours to protect her daughter from the fangs of a cruel and unrelenting tyrant, must suffer the penalty of the law! How long will a just and beneficent God withhold vengeance for such a violation of His law?—"How long, O Lord! how long?"

I will now conclude, by addressing a few words to the inhabitants of the only truly free country upon earth—Great Britain—that country which, even amid the din and tumult of war, contrived to find time and opportunity to put an end to the African slave-trade in the first place; and, latterly, while herself groaning beneath the burden of a debt which would have overwhelmed and annihilated any other European nation, nobly and generously devoted twenty millions sterling to the emancipation of her slaves in all parts of the world.

In the name of my oppressed race I appeal to you, noble and generous Britons, to stretch forth your hands, and assist in alleviating our condition.

You can at least give us your sympathy and your prayers; and, although we cannot ask you to interpose directly in our behalf, by interfering with the Government of America, you can, as individuals, and as associations combined for the abolition of slavery, address and remonstrate with your brethren in America. You can print and circulate pamphlets, both in Britain, and America, which, sooner or later, may arouse inquiry into the nature and effects of slavery amongst those who have hitherto beheld the unrighteous institution with apathy; and the more inquiry that is made, and the more that is learned, of the real condition of the negroes, the more will Christian and human sympathy be awakened in our favour.

The American Government have declared that they will not even receive petitions in behalf of the slave; but although, as public members of Congress, they may refuse to listen to our complaints and remonstrances, it may be that, as private citizens of America, they will not object to peruse arguments and documents which may be distributed, in the form of pamphlets, over the length and the breadth of the land. We would beseech you, then, generous Britons, as you prize and appreciate the blessings of liberty yourselves, to listen to our prayers. We have no means of petitioning *directly* the Government of America; and, even in those states which hold no slaves, there is yet a prejudice against the black race which does not exist in Britain. Mr. George Thompson, while visiting America, experienced cogent proofs of what I assert.

All that I ask, in the mean time, is this: that such of my readers as may have been interested in the facts and observations which I have laid before them, and who feel a benign spirit within them whisper something in behalf of Africa's sable sons, may exert their influence in calling the attention of their friends and acquaintances to the subject. I shall wait with patience, but with anxiety, to learn what effect, if

s

any, these pages may produce on the minds of men in Britain; and, if I should succeed in exciting a fresh interest in our behalf among the free sons of England, there is little doubt but that a similar feeling will in time extend to this side of the Atlantic. Perhaps some member of Congress may be induced to deliberate upon and investigate the question of slavery in all its bearings, and finally set on foot some agitation amongst his friends, to inquire whether or not Congress may not have been too rash in prohibiting the reception of any petition in behalf of slaves. " Behold how great a flame a little fire kindleth!" So, let it be hoped that Zamba's humble volume may yet advance the cause which he pleads.

To such of my readers as have gone thus far, allow me to return my most grateful thanks ; and, should the liberal-minded people of Britain, before whom I have ventured to appear, honour me with their approval and patronage on this occasion, and should circumstances otherwise warrant, I hope to be spared long enough to have the honour again to address them.

THE END.